The Complete Guide to

Weimaraners

Vanessa Richie

LP Media Inc. Publishing
Text copyright © 2023 by LP Media Inc.
All rights reserved.
No part of this book may be reproduced or transmitted in any form or by any means, electronic or mechanical, including photocopying, recording, or by an information storage and retrieval system – except by a reviewer who may quote brief passages in a review to be printed in a magazine or newspaper – without permission in writing from the publisher. For information address LP Media Inc. Publishing, 3178 253rd Ave. NW, Isanti, MN 55040
www.lpmedia.org

Publication Data
Vanessa Richie
The Complete Guide to Weimaraners – First edition.
Summary: "Successfully raising a Weimaraner dog from puppy to old age"
Provided by publisher.
ISBN: 978-1-954288-80-5
[1. The Complete Guide to Weimaraners – Non-Fiction] I. Title.

This book has been written with the published intent to provide accurate and authoritative information in regard to the subject matter included. While every reasonable precaution has been taken in preparation of this book the author and publisher expressly disclaim responsibility for any errors, omissions, or adverse effects arising from the use or application of the information contained inside. The techniques and suggestions are to be used at the reader's discretion and are not to be considered a substitute for professional veterinary care. If you suspect a medical problem with your dog, consult your veterinarian.
Design by Sorin Rădulescu
First hardcover edition, 2023

Table of Contents

Introduction 1

Part 1
Getting to Know the Weimaraner 3

Chapter 1
Is the Weimaraner Right for You? 4
Important Considerations 8
Adult Versus Puppy 9

Chapter 2
Breed History of the Weimaraner 15
A Big Dog for Big Game 16
The Nobleman's Dog 16
Joining the German Club 17
Surviving War 18
Gaining in Popularity 19
The Current Status of the Silver Ghost 20

Chapter 3
Weimaraner Attributes and Temperament 21
A Large, Ghostly Appearance 22

An Larger than Life Personality 24
Breed Standards 30

Part 2
Adopting and the Early Days with Your Weimaraner 31

Chapter 4
Finding Your Weimaraner 32
Ways to Get a Weimaraner 33
Rescuing a Weimaraner 34
Choosing a Weimaraner Breeder and Puppy 38

Chapter 5
Preparing Your Budget and Family for Your New Weimaraner 47
Planning the First Year's Budget 48
Instructing Your Children 51
Preparing Your Current Dogs and Cats 55

Chapter 6
Preparing Your Home and Schedule 59
Creating a Safe Space for Your Adult Dog or Puppy 61
Crates — An Absolute Essential for Weimaraners 62
Puppy-Proof/Dog-Proof the House 63
Choosing Your Veterinarian 70

Chapter 7
Bringing Your Weimaraner Home 73
Final Preparations and Planning.............................74
Picking up Your Puppy or Dog and the Ride Home............79
The First Vet Visit and What to Expect......................81
Crate and Other Preliminary Training 84
First-Night Frights 87

Chapter 8
Introducing Your Weimaraner to Your Other Dogs.....89
Introducing Your New Puppy to Your Other Pets...............90
Introducing an Adult Dog to Other Pets 93
Older Dogs and Your Weimaraner 94
Dog Aggression and Territorial Behavior.....................96
Feeding Time Practices......................................97

Chapter 9
The First Few Weeks 99
Setting the Rules and Sticking to Them..................... 101
Establish a No Jumping and No Mouthing Policy.............. 102
Reward-Based Training Versus Discipline-Based Training 106
How Long Is Too Long to Be Left Home Alone? 107
Don't Overdo It – Physically or Mentally 109

Part 3
Training and Activities 111

Chapter 10
House-training.. 112

Inside or Outside – House-training Options and Considerations 116

Reward Good Behavior with Positive Reinforcement 119

Cleaning Up 121

Chapter 11
Training Your Weimaraner 123

Early Training is a Must 125

Best Practices and Benefits to Keep in Mind before You Start... 126

Choosing the Right Reward 127

Name Recognition 128

Essential Commands 129

    Sit... 130

    Down.. 132

    Stay... 132

    Come.. 133

    Leave It 134

    Drop It.. 135

    Heel 136

    Off 138

Quiet 139
Where to Go from Here 139

Chapter 12
Socialization.. 143
Greeting New People.. 145
Greeting New Dogs... 146
The Importance of Continuing Socialization 147
Socializing an Adult Dog.. 148

Chapter 13
Playtime and Exercise 151
Exercise Needs 152
Outdoor Activities 154
Indoor Activities 163

Part 4
Taking Care of Your Weimaraner................................. 167

Chapter 14
Nutrition 168
Why a Healthy Diet is Important... 169
Dangerous Foods 170
Canine Nutrition.. 171
Different Dietary Requirements for Different
Life Stages... 175

Your Dog's Meal Options 178
Scheduling Meals 184
Food Allergies and Intolerance 184

Chapter 15
Grooming – Productive Bonding 185

Chapter 16
General Health Issues: Allergies, Parasites, and Vaccinations 197
The Role of Your Veterinarian 198
Allergies 199
Fleas and Ticks 201
Parasitic Worms 203
Vaccinating Your Weimaraner 207
Holistic Alternatives 208

Chapter 17
Genetic Health Concerns Common to the Weimaraner 209
Common Weimaraner Health Issues 210
Common Owner Mistakes 215
Prevention and Monitoring 216

Chapter 18
The Aging Weimaraner 217
Senior Care Challenges 219

Vet Visits.. 223
Changes to Watch for 224
Keeping Your Senior Dog Mentally Active....................... 227
Advantages to the Senior Years 228
Preparing to Say Goodbye 229
Grief and Healing 231

Introduction

Weimaraners are dogs that make a real first impression. The first thing you will notice is the unique silver color of their coats, which look more like velvet than fur. This will quickly be forgotten as the dog lets you know it's time to play. This is a dog that was carefully bred to be a fantastic hunting partner. While they are typically pets and companions these days, Weimaraners' energy levels and intellect remain incredibly high. This makes the breed ideal for active families who want a dog that can be just as engaged and enthusiastic as they are. Swimming, hiking, biking, jogging, exploring, and a whole host of other activities that you love are something that a Weimaraner can do and still have energy left over. It also means these dogs are not a good breed for people who have never had a dog or who live a more sedentary life.

The breed started with one man who wanted the perfect hunting dog. Ironically, the dog's coat was one of the few things that were not intentional. The original breeder, the Duke of Weimar, was focused on getting the right personality traits and physical attributes for hunting. Initially, the dogs joined in hunts for large game, particularly bears, boars, and deer. Over time, the dogs joined in more leisurely hunts for smaller game. As hunting became less common, the dogs transitioned to being pets like most other working dogs. Over that period of transition from big-game hunters to pets, the breed came to be known for their accidentally gorgeous coats. They are nicknamed Silver Ghosts or Gray Ghosts.

For a long time, this was a very exclusive breed. The breeding of different dogs was highly monitored, resulting in surprisingly healthy dogs. Weimaraners do have some ailments, but they have a longer life span than most large canines, living between 11 and 14 years.

These dogs get along well with children and other animals. Given their long hunting history, Weimaraners do have a strong prey drive, which means a lot of early training is necessary for puppies to keep them from trying to chase everything that moves. Fortunately, they love to please, making them easy to train. This should help to encourage you to keep up with training because a Weimaraner that is bored or doesn't get enough activity is a destructive dog. You will need to be patient when you train your dog, but Weimaraners respond very well to positive training early in the learning process.

These dogs are not a good breed for families who have no experience with dogs or for families with young children or elderly people in the home. Though fantastic pets, Weimaraners are high-energy dogs, and when they get excited, they are not very attentive to those around them. They won't mean to knock people over or hurt others, but it can happen. It is best to have a yard with a Weimaraner because it makes it much easier to manage the dog's natural energy and exuberance.

This book is divided into four sections.

Part 1 – Getting to Know the Weimaraner

This section provides basic information about the breed, including a brief history, a description of the breed's appearance, and its characteristics so that you can determine if this is the right kind of dog for you and your household.

Part 2 – Adopting and the Early Days with Your Weimaraner

These chapters will help you plan for your Weimaraner's arrival and help you map out your first month with your newest family member.

Part 3 – Training and Activities

In these chapters, we will help you understand the challenges you will face and provide the knowledge you will need to help you be successful in training your dog.

Part 4 – Taking Care of Your Weimaraner

These chapters cover how to take care of your Weimaraner's health, the breed's hereditary ailments, and the canine ailments that come with age.

PART 1

Getting to Know the Weimaraner

CHAPTER 1

Is the Weimaraner Right for You?

Weimaraners love to play and be a part of the family. They are considered Velcro dogs, meaning they want to stick to their people all of the time. If you are at home, your Weimaraner is going to be right there with you. These dogs don't like to be home alone, and given their high intelligence and boundless energy, they shouldn't be in a home where people are absent for most of the day. At least Weimaraners should have buddies to keep them company over the course of a day.

If you want a dog that is going to get you active, it is hard to do much better than a Weimaraner. They aren't going to try to compete with you or push you to do more. Instead, they are more like cheerleaders who want to do whatever you are doing. You'll need a big vehicle since they're large dogs, but you won't have to worry about your dog running out of steam during an activity.

Before they mature, Weimaraners take a significant amount of work because they will get fairly big (between 23 and 27 inches to their shoulders on average) and will have a lot of energy. These are dogs that typically do not slow down until old age. Once they are mature, they can be the perfect companion dogs, so long as they have been properly socialized and trained.

When asked what the right kind of home for a Weimaraner is, two breeders pointed out important elements of what would be a good fit:

A family willing to accept the fact there will be a new child in the house. Active, smart people who love a challenge and are willing to be creative.

> *A family willing to accept the fact there will be a new child in the house. Active, smart people who love a challenge and are willing to be creative.*
>
> **TONI FOW**
> *Wing It Weimaraners*
>
> *Weims thrive in active households where they get plenty of physical and mental activity. Ideally, the home has access to an area where the Weim can free run, use its nose, explore natural areas, and interact with the environment.*
>
> **ANNE TYSON**
> *Regen Weimaraners*

What's Great About Weimaraners	
A dedicated and loving member of the family	These dogs love their families. They will happily join in whatever fun and games your family is enjoying, and there are so many games you can play with a Weimaraner.
A fantastic exercise buddy	It's hard to find a better canine exercise buddy than the Weimaraner. They can join you on jogs and bike rides (though you have to wait until they are fully mature and their bones finish growing). They are fabulous when it comes to nearly every type of exercise, so you will have options for what you want to do any given day—and your Weimaraner will be happy with whatever you choose.
A gorgeous coat that's easy to tend	The Weimaraner's coat is gorgeous and surprisingly low maintenance. They do shed, but short hair doesn't collect nearly as much as the hair of many other breeds.
An athletic dog for athletic people	If you want a constant companion that will always work with your exercise schedule, you really can't beat the Weimaraner as an exercise buddy. That expression of sheer happiness, while you guys are active, is more than enough of an incentive to keep going.
A loyal, loving companion	This isn't a lounging dog, but after a busy day, your Weimaraner will be happy to recline. Bonding with these loyal dogs is easy and often doesn't take very long.
Protectors when needed	The Weimaraner may not be an aggressive breed, but if they see someone with bad intentions, they will protect their people. They have been used as police dogs and in defensive training because they do have hunting instincts that make them good at protecting against threats. Once a Weimaraner thinks the threat is gone, the dog is back to being a loving family dog.
The fluffy goofball	That gorgeous coat and stunning eyes make the dog look like a canine gentleman, but they are actually incredible goofballs. This comes from that nearly limitless energy and a desire to be close to their people.

Why A Weimaraner May Not Be Right for You	
Not a first dog	This is a dog that has boundless energy, a high intellect, and a desire to do activities. If you don't have experience with training a dog, the Weimaraner is not a good choice. They require a firm, patient, and consistent application of the rules. When you break the rules or allow something to slide, your dog is going to figure out how to get you to do that again. There are other breeds that are much easier to train for first-time dog parents.
Strong prey drive	This is a dog that was bred to pursue, and that drive is still very strong in Weimaraners. Given their size, this can be disastrous if the dog isn't properly trained.
Potential behavior issues	When they are young, Weimaraners need to be trained to keep them from jumping up on people because they grow fast, and that energy level kicks in early. They can be exuberant, rowdy, and destructive without proper training, something that is a much more serious issue with larger dogs. Since they tend to remain highly energetic well into adulthood, they absolutely must learn how to behave when they are young; otherwise, they can be difficult to control and may become destructive.
Daily vigorous exercise	If you don't like to exercise or be active, this is not the dog for you. People who want a larger dog to lounge with them have plenty of choices, but the Weimaraner is not one of them.
Destructive when alone	Weimaraners do not do well when left alone for long periods of time. That high energy and intellect mean they get bored quickly, and this is often taken out on your home. Furniture (and other things) will be chewed if a Weimaraner is left alone and bored for hours.
Some bark – often	When a Weimaraner gets lonely or bored, barking may occur. The Weimaraner bark is not a deep boom but more of a higher sound that is easier to hear when hunting. That means their voice is loud and not entirely pleasant when you hear it often. This is another reason why you need to train your Weimaraner—you don't want your dog to bark at every sound that happens outside.

Why A Weimaraner May Not Be Right for You	
Not always great with smaller animals	Given their strong prey drive, without substantial training and socialization, your Weimaraner may not be great with smaller animals like cats and rodents or maybe even some smaller dogs. This is a hunting breed, and that is likely to come out if you don't teach the dog early that these little creatures are friends, not prey.

Important Considerations

One of the reasons that people love well-established breeds is that you pretty much know what you are going to get, regardless of the age of the dog. This will help you to plan for the different stages of the dog's life. Socialization can help minimize some behaviors, but older dog breeds are largely set in their ways. The usual temperament of the Weimaraner is good, but if untrained or unsocialized, you could be setting yourself up for failure with this breed. Here's what you can expect from your Weimaraner.

One dog breeder summed up what a Weimaraner needs from its people to be safe for both the dog and the family:

> *Own home, fenced yard, no children under five years. No owner over 60 years, safe place for dog when at work, previous dog owner, willing to do some kind of dog training classes (preferably fun ones)!*
>
> CHRISTINE GRISELL
> *Nani's Weimaraners*

This may seem like a lot of specific needs, but that's because the Weimaraner requires a lot of activity to be the amazing pet that people want. You want a breeder who is picky because that means they are more careful and caring for the puppies, and those puppies will have a much better foundation.

Adult Versus Puppy

The final question to ask yourself before you settle on a particular breed is whether you should get an adult or a puppy. The answer varies based on the individual or family. Probably the biggest consideration is size. You will need to regularly adjust collars and crates to accommodate a growing puppy. Adult dogs will require more monitoring when they are around other people and pets until you know their personality and temperament. Weimaraners are a good-natured breed, but without proper training and socialization, their size can make them more dangerous than smaller dogs, so you need to be prepared to quickly earn your new dog's respect and be very mindful of him for the first year.

Here are some considerations to help you determine which age dog is a better fit for your home.

Bringing Home an Adult Weimaraner

> *The benefit of getting an older dog is that you know more about its temperament from the start, so choose a dog that fits your lifestyle.*
>
> ANNE TYSON
> *Regen Weimaraners*

As mentioned earlier, you need to be careful and really consider if you can handle adopting an adult; if the dog is not properly trained, life can turn into a real struggle because of your new canine's stubbornness. Since Weimaraners are so big, they can also be rough, even if they don't mean to be. They can also be destructive if they don't get enough mental and physical exercise, and they can reach a lot higher and farther than most other breeds. You need to plan to start training from the moment you bring home the dog because even if your new Weimaraner has been trained, you still have to prove you are someone who should be listened to. Essentially, you have to prove you are a worthy leader, just

Chapter 1: Is the Weimaraner Right for You?

like you would at a new job, and that means being patient, positive, and kind, along with being firm and consistent.

If you have young children at home, you will need to watch your dog closely and make sure he has a positive reaction to kids, especially if you don't know the dog's history. You should also be careful about introducing a Weimaraner to other pets because this is not a breed that tends to do well with other animals if not introduced early. Weimaraners also may have difficulty with another dog that is the same gender, regardless of breed.

Adult dogs can give you more immediate gratification. You don't have to go through the sleepless nights that come with a new puppy. The odds are also that you aren't going to be starting from the beginning with house-training.

Photo Courtesy of Rebecca Carnes

Additionally, adult dogs are awake during the day a lot more than puppies, and while it may take your new dog a bit longer to warm up to you, you can still bond much faster with an adult.

Finally, one of the biggest benefits of acquiring an adult dog is that it will already be its full size. There is no need to guess how big your dog will grow to be, and that makes it easier to purchase the appropriate-sized gear and supplies right from the start.

The following is a list of questions to consider when adopting an adult Weimaraner:

- **Can you properly dog-proof your home before the dog arrives?**

You can't simply bring a dog into your home, whether an adult or a puppy, and let him run around unchecked. To be sure he learns the rules of the house before he is allowed to roam freely, you will need to have a safe, dedicated space for your new dog. (Details of how to dog-proof your home are discussed in Chapter 5.) It will take a lot more to dog-proof your home with a large breed because they can easily access things on top of counters, cabinets, and areas that are out of reach to most dogs.

> **FUN FACT**
>
> **Weimaraner Club of America (WCA)**
>
> Founded in 1943 in Boston, MA, the Weimaraner Club of America (WCA) is dedicated to preserving and protecting the interest of this breed. As the American Kennel Club-recognized parent club for Weimaraners in America, this club sponsors numerous annual events. For more information about club-sponsored events or becoming a member, visit www.weimaranerclubofamerica.org.

- **Do you have pets that will be affected by a new dog?**

Weimaraners have to be trained young to coexist with other animals. If they aren't trained and socialized when they are young, it is best not to bring them around other pets. This means you will need to know the history of an adult before bringing the dog home to a house with a cat or dog. If you plan to bring home a puppy, training and socializing will need to be a top priority for the safety of your puppy and your other pets.

- **What is the dog's health history?**

A complete health record for a rescued Weimaraner may not be available, but it is likely you will find a dog that has already been spayed or neutered as well as chipped. Unless you adopt a Weimaraner with health issues, which should be disclosed by the rescue organization (if known), rescues tend to be less costly than puppies at their first visit to the vet. In other words, for the first few years, your Weimaraner's health care visits should not be too expensive.

Bringing Home a Weimaraner Puppy

> *Some of the important tips in choosing a Weimaraner would be to see the facility in which the dog(s) are being raised. If purchasing a puppy, I would want to see the parents. Also, ask how long they have been breeding for.*
>
> JOE WIDOMSKI
> *Shade of Grey Weimaraners*

Puppies are a major time investment, and a dog as intelligent, large, and energetic as the Weimaraner will make some aspects of raising a puppy that much harder. How much time can you devote to a puppy's care? Will you be able to deal with an excitable puppy that has everything to learn and quickly becomes a puppy in a very large body?

A puppy will be a better fit if you can put in dedicated time for training and socializing before the dog becomes set in his ways. If you have other pets at home, a puppy is definitely a better choice than an adult because he is young and can be trained to follow your rules. (The exception would be if you find an adult that is already well-socialized.)

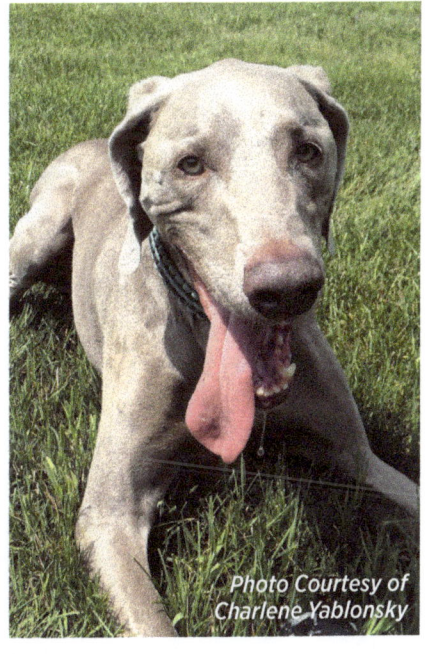
Photo Courtesy of Charlene Yablonsky

When determining whether or not a Weimaraner puppy is a good fit for your home, ask yourself:

- **How much time do you have available for training and socialization?**

All puppies are a lot of work, starting with the moment the puppy enters your care. While the Weimaraner's temperament is fairly predictable, how you train and socialize your puppy will affect every aspect of the dog's adult life. Training and socializing can take up a large chunk of time in the beginning, but both are absolutely essential for raising a healthy, well-mannered Weimaraner.

- **Are you able to show firmness and consistency when training?**

From the very start, you have to establish yourself and your family as the ones in charge; your Weimaraner must understand his place in the family hierarchy. You will need to be patient and consistent with your training, no matter how frustrated you may become or how cute those puppy eyes are. All intelligent dogs have a streak of stubbornness!

- **Do you have the time, energy, and budget to puppy-proof your home?**

The preparation for your puppy's arrival begins long before he first sets foot in your house. Puppy-proofing your home is as time-consuming as childproofing your home. If you do not have the time for this, then you should consider getting an adult dog. (Details of how to puppy-proof your home are discussed in Chapter 6.)

You will receive records about the puppy and the puppy's parents, which will make it easier to identify any health problems your Weimaraner might experience in the future. This makes it considerably easier to keep your puppy healthy and spot potential issues before they become major problems.

Chapter 1: Is the Weimaraner Right for You?

Some people find it easier to bond with puppies than with adult dogs. A young puppy may be nervous in a new home, but most adjust quickly because they are predisposed to enjoying the company of those around them.

Photo Courtesy of Trichelle Mattas

CHAPTER 2

Breed History of the Weimaraner

The unique appearance of the Weimaraner is a nod to the high-class roots of the breed. Bred by one man for years, then moving out to just a small group of breeders with tight control over the dog meant it was a highly exclusive dog for a long time.

A Big Dog for Big Game

> *Originally bred in European countries for hunting large and small game—think deer, wild boar, wolf, fox, rabbit, and birds—Weimaraners will dig under and jump over fences if they want to get at something badly enough; unfortunately, this also can include squirrels and cats. Some dogs can easily dig one to two feet and jump five to six feet.*
>
> KYRA SCHLIEMAN
> *SilverLining Weimaraners*

Some historians have pointed to a picture painted back in 1533 as the first signs of Weimaraners, with a large, light-colored dog standing next to King Charles V. This was an early ancestor to the breed, and they have periodically popped up in pictures and statues over the years.

The breeding of the first Weimaraners is thought to have begun during the 1850s in Weimar, which is in modern-day central Germany. The aristocracy enjoyed hunting and big-game sports, and they wanted a dog that would be able to accompany them. Setters and Pointers were great dogs for hunting, and they were used in the early breeding of the dog that eventually became the Weimaraner. One of the men most closely associated with the efforts was Prince Hans von Ratibor. Whatever records he kept were lost when he died, so there isn't much that is known about the first dogs or what he accomplished.

The Nobleman's Dog

By 1880, the Germanic aristocracy was familiar with the dog that had come to be known as the Silver Ghost, and some of them decided to enter their unique-looking dogs in the Berlin Show. The next year, the first litter that some consider pure Weimaraners was born.

Photo Courtesy of Trichelle Mattas

Those few who were fortunate enough to have this impressive dog were very careful with their breeding habits, keeping close records of their dogs and the results of breeding. To ensure their dogs remained healthy, the breeders were not willing to breed the dogs outside of a very small circle. This kept the dogs from losing the desired traits that had led to them being bred.

Major von Bunau was the first person to set forth breed standards for the Weimaraner, which he provided in 1896. At the time, there was a longhaired dog that was similar in appearance, and this sparked a debate about whether the Weimaraner actually was its own unique breed or if it was just a different color of the German Shorthaired Pointer. Ultimately, those saying it was a separate breed were successful, and the Weimaraner began to be officially acknowledged.

Joining the German Club

On June 20, 1897, the Club for the Pure Breeding of the Silver-grey Weimaraner Vorstehund was founded, later changed to the Society for the Breeding of the Weimaraner-Vorstehund.

As the foundation for early Weimaraners' health was incredibly controlled, this ensured a much healthier breed than many other purebred dogs. There were some changes and additions to the breed, with a longhaired Weimaraner being a version that gained some notoriety. However, the shorthaired Weimaraner was far more common and continues to be popular because it is so much easier to groom. Since this is a very active breed that loves to be outside, a shorthaired Weimaraner is far easier to manage.

Surviving War

People outside of Germany and Austria were interested in acquiring their own Weimaraners, particularly since the dog proved to be so essential to the sportsmen who had them. Howard Knight, an avid sportsman from New England, had seen the dogs and decided he wanted to have some. The only way to get a Weimaraner at that time was to apply to join the club. The club sent him two sterilized dogs. Unwilling to give up an effort to be able to breed his own dogs, Knight continued to press the group for dogs that were not fixed.

His efforts finally paid off in 1938. It's possible the club may have relented because of the looming war. During that year, Knight was given four dogs, most of them puppies—sisters Adda and Dorle von Schwarzen Kamp, Aura von Gaiberg, and Mars as der Wulfsreide. With the club becoming more willing to send dogs outside of Germany and Austria, there was a growing demand, particularly in the US.

Photo Courtesy of Stacey Perez

HISTORICAL FACT
American Origins

Originally bred as hunting dogs for German nobility, the first Weimaraners made their way to America in the 1920s. A Rhode Island businessman, Howard Knight, brought a couple of Weimaraners home to America in the 1920s, hoping to breed them. Unfortunately, the female was sterile, but Knight was able to import four more dogs in 1938, four years before the American Kennel Club (AKC) recognized Weimaraners as a breed. In addition to bringing Weimaraners to America, Knight was also the first American to become a member of the exclusive Weimaraner Club of Germany in 1929. Weimaraners are now the 44th most popular breed registered with the AKC.

By 1942, a new club was formed in the US called the Weimaraner Club of America. They submitted an application to the American Kennel Club (AKC) to get the breed recognized in the US. The AKC took only a few months, approving the breed by the end of the year that the application was submitted.

Weimaraners were far from the only breed that became incredibly popular in the US during the 1940s, and the period has been identified as a significant period for European dogs to be imported into the US. Many German breeds made their way to the US, as well as many breeds from France, England, and other nations embroiled in World War II.

Gaining in Popularity

As more people began to see this impressive-looking dog, it grew in popularity across North America. Initially, the dog did incredibly well in dog shows, often dominating at the top of the winner's podium. This led to the dog becoming a status symbol for many people without those people taking the time to learn about the Weimaraners before bringing the dog into their homes.

Unfortunately, this kind of popularity and perceived status led to lax breeding by people who were more interested in money than in the breed and its health. This resulted in a significant rise in health issues in the breed, as well as dogs that had bad tempers. As more dogs were

Chapter 2: Breed History of the Weimaraner

born with problems, the market became flooded with free Weimaraners because the cost of tending the dogs was too high, and the price people were willing to pay decreased.

Not all breeders were irresponsible, though. There were a number of Americans who wanted to help maintain the high standards established by the club, and they strictly controlled the breeding of their dogs to ensure the pups were healthy and good-tempered. It took about a decade, but as the popularity of the breed waned, the people who continued to breed them were the ones who were more attentive to the standards and health. They actively worked to fix the problems and brought back the healthy, happy dog people know and love today.

Photo Courtesy of Jeff Daugherty

The Current Status of the Silver Ghost

In the early part of the 21st century, Weimaraners again began to become popular. They are in the top 50 most popular dogs in the US. Following the boom and loss of breeding standards, breeders today are being much more careful about breeding their dogs so that Weimaraners can continue to thrive and be healthy, active dogs. Unlike a lot of other purebred dogs, the Weimaraner has a robust community of breeders who are more interested in their dogs' health, which is a significant contributor to them being large dogs with a longer life expectancy. This is what has made the Silver Ghost such a popular choice for families. This is a dog that is very much a member of the family, and having one encourages people to be more active.

CHAPTER 3

Weimaraner Attributes and Temperament

Weimaraners have a similar build to many other dogs, but their coat makes them entirely unique in the canine world. That appearance hides a personality that makes this a dog that is very much one of a kind. With roots as hunters, they've changed with the times to become the kind of dog that will happily join weekend warriors out looking to cram as much activity into the weekend as possible. They are great for families who like to go outside and do things together. And they are all-around great dogs when they are in a home that can accommodate that large personality.

A Large, Ghostly Appearance

Since they chased large prey in their early history, Weimaraners are big. With their silver coats, they look a bit like ghosts racing across the landscape. Their sleek bodies were built for the chase. Their color meant they were harder to see, even if that feature was incidental. Their bark isn't the full-throated bark of most working dogs. It is more like the bark of a Husky or Dalmatian so that they can be quickly located during the hunt. When they get excited (which is often), their stubby little tail moves so rapidly it is hard to miss.

There is no dog quite like a Weimaraner.

A Trim Frame

There are some differences in the Weimaraner body, but all standards require a very trim frame (the European standard just looks a bit more muscular than the American standards). They range in weight from 55 to 90 lbs., so they have been classified as both medium- and large-sized dogs. However, they are typically considered large dogs since medium-sized dogs are traditionally between 20 and 60 lbs. Their height puts them in the same range

> **HELPFUL TIP**
> **Ready, Set, Action!**
>
> Weimaraners are famously high-energy dogs with intensive exercise needs. A happy Weimaraner is a well-exercised Weimaraner. As a result, these dogs especially enjoy agility training and make ideal running companions. When choosing a Weimaraner for your home, plan for an average of two hours of daily exercise with your pup. If your Weimaraner is getting enough exercise, he'll happily spend much of his day relaxing around your home.

as German Shorthaired Pointers, Foxhounds, Dalmatians, Rhodesian Ridgebacks, and Doberman Pinschers.

The thin frame is common to athletic dogs that are great runners. This is absolutely true of the Weimaraner, though they run more for distance than speed. They should keep this trim frame to stay healthy. You should be able to see where the rib cage ends, although you shouldn't be able to see each individual rib. It's a fine balance when it comes to keeping a Weimaraner (or any dog with this build) healthy since they are very much food motivated.

A Regal Face

Weimaraners have a very serious, aristocratic look to them. The long floppy ears can arch on their heads in a way that highlights the finer points of their faces. Given the unique color of the breed, their blue, amber, or gray eyes really stand out, giving the dog a haunting look. If you don't know their typical temper and personality, they can look very

Photo Courtesy of April James

intimidating as they watch you expectantly. The long snout has jowls that hide their teeth, leaving the length of those teeth to the imagination. That said, the dogs have a tendency to be goofy, and they will often do something that looks decidedly unregal within minutes of meeting people.

> **FUN FACT**
> **Baby Blues**
>
> Weimaraner puppies are born with striking blue or gray eyes. As they grow, however, their eyes become darker due to melanin production. As a result, adult Weimaraners typically have gray, amber, or blueish-gray eyes.

The Pale, Ghostly Coat

This is usually what people notice first about the dog. The coat of a Weimaraner looks like velvet, making people want to reach out and touch it to see if it is as soft as it looks.

Their coats come in several shades, from mouse-gray to silver, but some Weimaraners have coats with other colors, usually more bluish, black, or a unique brownish-red. These colors typically disqualify dogs from shows. Since the fur is short, the coat is also very sleek. However, it doesn't have the kind of coarse texture typically associated with short-haired canines.

Some dogs have white spots, with one on the chest being fairly common. Otherwise, they are typically one solid color that is not seen with nearly any other breed.

An Larger than Life Personality

Weimaraners have a lot of love to give, and that is backed by an exuberance that seems limitless. Loyal, loving, goofy, and energetic are terms often associated with this breed. Despite a history as hunting dogs, they are generally very affable and welcoming, though that desire to chase is still very strong in the dogs. It also helps them to be fairly fearless.

A Loving, Affectionate Breed

When you have a Velcro dog, you have to understand that personal space simply doesn't exist with them. This is both because they love you so much and because they don't want to miss anything. Since they want to be with you all of the time, they also want to meet everyone you meet and engage in social activities with you.

A Good Watchdog, Poor Guard Dog

> *The breed being very intelligent and stubborn can be both easy and difficult to train. My spouse, of German descent himself, likes to say, 'You have to say NO one more time than the dog wants to hear it.' But of course, with consistency and love!*
>
> **KYRA SCHLIEMAN**
> *SilverLining Weimaraners*

If push comes to shove, a Weimaraner will protect the pack. The problem is that this is a friendly, outgoing breed that prefers to be happy and friendly. They have to perceive something to be a threat, which is a much higher threshold for Weimaraners than the typical German guard dog. If you want a guard dog, the German Shepherd or any one of many other breeds is a much better fit. At best, Weimaraners are reluctant protectors, mostly because they are more lovers than fighters.

Their high levels of energy mean they are prone to being restless. With their large ears, they also hear a lot more than we do. So, if there are sounds outside that catch your Weimaraner's interest, there is a very high likelihood that your dog is going to let you know. With their high voices, you won't be able to miss his bark either.

A High-Energy Dog, High-Intelligence Breed

Weimaraners can be great jogging companions because they aren't prone to overheating, or they can go swimming because they are fantastic swimmers. They can learn how to jog next to you as you bike. Then there are dog activities that can really engage them, like agility training and coursing.

The high intellect combined with the desire to please means they are generally easy to train, as long as they understand they aren't the pack leaders. You can teach Weimaraners so many tricks. For example, they can learn to give hugs (something they will love because you are allowing them to invade your personal space).

The downside to the high-energy, high-intellect Weimaraner is that boredom is a constant concern. If they don't get both enough exercise and adequate mental stimulation, they will come up with their own activities. This is typically going to be detrimental to your stuff, your home, and your ears. They can be prolific barkers when they are bored, even if they have been trained. From chasing animals to escaping your yard, it is too risky to leave this breed outside without supervision. Not only can they dig under your fence, but they are smart enough to figure out how to get over the top of the fence (which is usually a lot faster than digging).

Training Is Essential, Especially with Smaller Children and Dogs

Until a Weimaraner is fully trained and knows how to safely interact with children and smaller dogs, it is best not to have the dog around them. Weimaraners are simply unaware of their size and the potential

Photo Courtesy of Lisa Shriver

harm they can do to smaller creatures. With smaller kids, the dog is likely to bowl them over. With smaller dogs, the Weimaraner is likely to feel that a smaller canine's desire to put some distance between them is an invitation to chase. A lot of training is essential to ensuring the safety of all parties. Socialization is also vital, but even after being socialized, a Weimaraner may get a little too excited, in which case you need to make sure the dog will listen to you when you want him to calm down.

Playful and Enthusiastic

> *Lots of running! Especially if you have a heavy field pedigree, these types need to run daily— not just yard play, but to run for miles in a field or on a leash, or lots of rambunctious play with other dogs. A tired Weim is a good Weim! Most destructive or annoying behaviors are due to a lack of exercise ... tire them out daily. They make fabulous running partners!*
>
> JESSICA HANSON
> *Hanson Weimaraners*

    This is a dog that pretty much wants to play all of the time. Yes, this can get a bit annoying when you want to relax, but it also means you have someone that is more than happy to help you feel better after a rough day or when you are feeling down.

    If you are the kind of person who requires a bit of gentle encouragement to go out and exercise or to be more active, the Weimaraner will give you a lot of reasons to go out and experience life. They are a fantastic workout partner for anything cardio-related, and they will love exploring new places with you. Their enthusiasm is contagious, and that can make even a dull run of errands feel more exciting. It's just easier to see the positive things around you when you have such an enthusiastic dog eager to have fun with you.

Photo Courtesy of Kimberly Marx

Breed Standards

The Weimaraner is a dog that seems to inspire a lot of passion in the people who love them, and many clubs have spawned around the Weimaraner. Although very similar, the standards for a Weimaraner in the UK have some differences from the AKC standard. And both of these are a bit different compared to the standards of the Weimaraner Club of America. Of course, all of these are different compared to the official standards of the original club. If you plan to put your Weimaraner in dog shows, you will need to check the standards that apply for that show.

The official breed standard in Europe includes the longer-haired version, as well as the very muscular shorthaired version. You can review the full standard on the Federation Cynologique Internationale site at (http://www.fci.be/Nomenclature/Standards/099g07-en.pdf). It is a long document with a lot of attention to the appearance and temperament of the dog. The document gives a fairly comprehensive look at the breed.

Since the Weimaraner Club was established and working toward the American standard of the breed before the AKC had recognized the breed, it may be best to consult their standards first. The Weimaraner Club of America has a very easy-to-read guide on the breed standards for most of North America (https://weimaranerclubofamerica.org/illustrated_standard.php). The full page has illustrations and a breakdown based on the dog's gender (males are larger than females). The AKC also has a much shorter version of the standards that they keep for the breed on their site (https://images.akc.org/pdf/breeds/standards/Weimaraner.pdf).

PART 2

Adopting and the Early Days with Your Weimaraner

CHAPTER 4

Finding Your Weimaraner

Weimaraners are fairly costly over the course of their lives because they are larger dogs that love to be busy. Rescuing an adult Weimaraner will initially be less costly, but you will probably get far less information about the dog's breeding history, training, and socialization. Surprisingly, puppies are not nearly as expensive as a lot of other purebred dogs, usually starting at around $700 and capping off by $1,700; it's harder to get an average price for rescues because the cost varies depending on the area. Typically, it will be a few hundred dollars.

You should also consider all of the items you need to purchase prior to your new family member coming home. Weimaraners will need big beds, big crates, big bowls, and big collars. If you bring home a puppy, you will have even more costs because you will probably have a much smaller crate and other items in the beginning; then, you will need to scale up as your dog quickly grows from a cute little puppy into a large, gangly adolescent.

Ways to Get a Weimaraner

This chapter is broken into two primary sections: rescuing a Weimaraner and adopting a Weimaraner. Typically, people rescue an adult, and they adopt a puppy.

- Dog rescues are one of the most reliable ways to get a healthy adult Weimaraner. The rescuers tend to go above and beyond to ensure the health of the dog.
- Shelters are usually not dedicated to any one breed. However, that doesn't mean you can't find a Weimaraner or a dog that has a lot of Weimaraner genetics and that lovable, enthusiastic temperament.

While you can get puppies from both rescue organizations and shelters, it is more likely that you will find a puppy from one of the following sources:

- Breeders are the most reliable source for purebred dogs, but you have to be careful. Puppy mills focus on producing as many dogs as possible for the lowest cost. They are far less likely to do

- any testing and screening, so their dogs are more likely to have genetic problems.
- Pet stores may get their dogs from a puppy mill. They also aren't likely to get their dogs from great breeders (breeders who really take care of their dogs are far more likely to be picky about who adopts their puppies).

You can find rescued puppies from puppy mills and pet stores at a dog rescue group or pet shelter. You can also get a great adult dog from a breeder, especially if a breeder takes one of their dogs back from a client who did not follow the contract. Sometimes people have to surrender their dogs, and breeders often prefer to have their dogs returned to them so they can find another good home for the dog.

To find your perfect Weimaraner, make sure to check multiple avenues unless you want a puppy, in which case a breeder is probably your best bet.

Rescuing a Weimaraner

This is a breed that tends to have a lot of specialized rescue centers around North America. If you run a quick search in your area, you may find there is one near you. Should you find there isn't a Weimaraner rescue in your local area, here are a few websites that can help you find a Weimaraner or Weimaraner mix to adopt:

- Weimaraner Rescue Directory (https://justweimaraners.com/weimaraner-rescue-directory/) – This is probably the next place to go to if you can't locate a local agency because you will very likely find someone close, regardless of where you are in the US.
- 6 Best Weimaraner Rescues in the US (2023) (https://welovedoodles.com/weimaraner-rescues/)
- Oregon and Washington Weimaraner Rescue (https://www.oregonweimrescue.org)
- Great Lakes Weimaraner Rescue (https://greatlakesweimrescue.com)

- Weimaraner Rescue of the South (https://www.oregonweimrescue.org)
- Florida Weimaraner Rescue (https://www.bdrr.org/weimaraner)
- Weimaraner Rescue of Texas (https://www.weimrescuetexas.org)

As one breeder pointed out:

> *The rescue group usually has information on why a dog was turned into the rescue. Talk to the person that is caring for the rescue to find out about issues!*
>
> **CHRISTINE GRISELL**
> *Nani's Weimaraners*

If you can't find a rescue near your home, you can also contact Weimaraner breeders to see if they have had any of their puppies returned that are at least two years old. That way, the breeders will have a better understanding of the dog and its personality, and they will be able to answer any future questions you might have. Keep in mind the following questions when adopting a Weimaraner:

- What is the reason the dog was surrendered?
- Did the dog have any health issues when he arrived?
- Do they know how the dog was treated by the previous family? What kind of training was he given? Was he mistreated? Was he socialized?
- How many homes has the dog experienced?
- What kind of veterinary care did the dog receive? Are there records that confirm this?
- Will the dog require extra medical attention based on known or suspected problems?
- Is the dog house-trained?

- How well does the dog react to strangers while walking in unfamiliar areas?
- Does the dog tend to be aggressive or guard his food when eating?
- How does the dog react to children and to other dogs and pets?
- Does the dog have any known allergies?
- Does the dog have any known dietary restrictions?
- If there are problems with the dog after adoption, will the organization take him back?

You should always meet an adult dog before adopting and bringing the dog home. As one breeder pointed out when asked about rescue Weimaraners:

> *For a rescue, meet the dog and make sure it is the right fit for your household. The benefit of getting an older dog is that you know more about its temperament from the start, so choose a dog that fits your lifestyle.*
>
> ANNE TYSON
> *Regen Weimaraners*

Types of Rescues

It is possible that you will find a Weimaraner in a shelter or through a more traditional rescue group because this is, unfortunately, a breed that people often get without understanding just how active the dog is. This means it is more likely for this dog to be abandoned because people simply don't want to work with it or can't meet the dog's exercise needs. If you do find a dog through these organizations, you almost certainly will not be able to get documentation about the dog's breeding, training, and socialization. Also, the dog likely won't be well trained.

Rescue and Shelter Adoption Requirements

Adopting an adult is significantly different from adopting a puppy. Since the dogs have already been to at least one home prior to being brought into a rescue, diligent rescues want to make sure their dogs go to a home that is willing and able to take care of their dogs, minimizing the likelihood that they will be returned. When a rescue group is dedicated to a breed, they will have different, more breed-specific methods of handling and taking care of the dogs. There are no rescue requirements or standards that apply everywhere. Some require home visits, though this tends to be fairly rare. Others have requirements for what you have to do within a set amount of time after your dog goes home with you.

In the US, many of the shelter requirements are based on state laws. The website NomNom has created a page that details the requirements for those living in the US, https://www.nomnomnow.com/learn/article/pet-adoption-laws-by-state.

With a breed like the Weimaraner, you may have more success asking breeders if they have an adult or returned dog instead of looking for the rare rescues that specialize in Weimaraners. Many breeders require puppies or dogs to be returned to them if the adopting family is unable to continue to take care of the dog, so they may have one or two adults they are willing to adopt out. Their requirements for adopting a returned dog will be different from adopting a dog from a rescue group.

You should be able to visit the facility and meet the rescue Weimaraner. A really good rescue will want to be involved in the process and will help determine if your home is a good fit for a particular dog. Since they know the dog well, they will be a pretty good judge of if the dog

HISTORICAL FACT
Tail Docking and Dew Claws

Historically Weimaraners have had their tails docked and dew claws removed. Initially, this modification was performed as a safety measure for these dogs, allowing them to avoid injury while performing duties related to hunting. Today, a docked tail and dewclaw removal remain part of the breed standard and are supported by the WCA and AKC so long as these modifications are made by a "skilled practitioner."

is a good fit for your home—and this is a good sign because it means they are interested in making sure the dog doesn't need to be rehomed again.

Choosing a Weimaraner Breeder and Puppy

> *Look for a breeder who is responsive to your questions in a timely manner, generally one to three business days via email or phone contact. They should welcome your questions, but generally will look for potential owners who have done their 'homework' on the breed. Choose a breeder that is knowledgeable about the good and bad health issues, personality, activity, and temperament characteristics of the Weimaraner. Good breeders should care deeply about the puppies they have produced, and as such will have questions for you to assure them that you understand the breed and can care for the dog adequately throughout its life.*
>
> **KYRA SCHLIEMAN**
> *SilverLining Weimaraners*

Finding a responsible breeder is the best thing you can do for your puppy because good breeders work only with healthy Weimaraner parents, which reduces the odds of serious genetic health issues. Weimaraners typically cost between $700 and $1,700, depending on where the breeder is located and how long they've been established. While cost is important, it is far more important to assess the breeder to ensure you get a healthy dog.

Always take the time to do your research. Although breeders for Weimaraners are largely reputable, you might run across an individual who is more interested in making a lot of money than in caring for the dogs. The goal is to locate breeders who are willing to answer ALL of your questions patiently and thoroughly. They should show as much love for their Weimaraners as they expect you to show for your new puppy; their goal should be to locate good homes for all of their animals.

Photo Courtesy of Dawna Miller

It is a particularly good sign if you find a breeder who posts pictures and information about the dog's parents, documents the progress of the mother's pregnancy, and shares descriptions of all vet visits. The best breeders will also stay in contact with you and answer any questions that might arise after you take the puppy home. Taking an active interest in what happens to the puppies in their new homes shows that breeders care a great deal about each individual dog.

You also want to find a breeder who is willing to talk about problems that might develop with your Weimaraner. Good breeders will ensure the adopting family is capable of properly socializing and training their Weimaraner.

It is likely that your conversation with each breeder will last about an hour. Make sure you take careful notes during every interview. If a breeder does not have time to talk when you call and isn't willing to call you back—cross them off your list!

The following are some questions to consider when researching breeders:

- Ask if you can visit in person. The answer should always be yes, and if it isn't, you don't need to ask anything further. Thank the breeder and hang up. Even if the breeder is located in a different state, they should always allow you to visit their facility.
- Ask about the health tests and certifications breeders have for their puppies. (These points are detailed further in the next section, so make sure to check off the available tests and certifications with every breeder.) If they don't have all of the tests and certifications, remove the breeder from your list of considerations.
- Make sure the breeder takes care of the initial health requirements, particularly shots, for each puppy from the first few weeks of birth through the dog's early months. Vaccinations and worming typically start at around six weeks of age and should be continued every three weeks. By the time your puppy is old enough to come home with you, he should be well into the first phase of these procedures or be completely finished with these important health care needs.
- Ask if the puppy is required to be spayed or neutered before reaching a certain age.
- Inquire whether or not the breeder is part of a Weimaraner organization or group.
- Ask about the first phases of your puppy's life, such as how the breeder will take care of the puppy before it goes home with you. They should be able to provide a lot of details, and they should not sound irritated by your questioning. They should also explain what training your puppy will receive prior to leaving the facility. It is possible the breeder might start house-training your puppy. If so, ask about the puppy's progress so that you know where to pick up training once your Weimaraner reaches your home.
- Breeders should be more than happy to help guide you in doing what is best for your dog because they want their puppies to live happy, healthy lives. You should also be able to rely on any recommendations your breeder makes about taking your puppy home, particularly about the first days of living with the puppy.

- Ask how many varieties of dogs the breeder manages in one year and how many sets of parent dogs they own. Mother dogs should have some downtime between pregnancies before producing another litter. Learn about breeders' standard operations to be sure they take care of the parents and treat them as valuable family members—not strictly as a way to make money.

Photo Courtesy of Trichelle Mattas

Ask about aggression in the puppy's parents and find out if there are other dogs in the breeder's home. While a puppy's temperament is more malleable than an adult's, some exposure to other breeds might make it easier when integrating the puppy into a home that already has dogs. Aggression isn't a normal problem for Weimaraners, but if you have smaller animals in your home, this will be important to know.

Don't be worried about getting a little personal. Just as the breeder should have an interest in finding the right home for their puppies, you should be looking for a breeder who has a love for the breed. Here are some questions you can ask to get a better idea of a breeder's motivations.
- Why did you choose to breed Weimaraners?
- Are the sire and dam AKC champions?
- What do you look for in a new home for the puppies?

You want to have an open and transparent conversation to make sure that not only are you a good home for a Weimaraner but that the breeders are a good fit for breeding and handling the puppies at their most vulnerable.

Contracts and Guarantees

> *Breeders should belong to our parent club, The Weimaraner Club of America, whose code of ethics guidelines help ensure the protection and advancement of the Weimaraner. It is a wonderful resource for anyone interested in the Weimaraner.*
>
> KYRA SCHLIEMAN
> *SilverLining Weimaraners*

Breeder contracts and guarantees are meant to protect the puppies as much as they are meant to protect you. If a breeder has a contract, make sure you read through it completely and are willing to meet all of the requirements prior to signing. Contracts tend to be fairly easy to understand and comply with, but you should be aware of all the facts before you agree to anything. Signing the contract indicates you are serious about committing to giving your puppy the best care possible and to meeting the minimum care requirements set forth by the breeder.

A contract may state the breeder will retain the puppy's original registration papers, although you will receive a copy of the papers too.

If a family does not meet all requirements as stated in the contract, it is the breeder's responsibility to remove the puppy from the family. These are the dogs some breeders offer for adoption.

A guarantee states the kind of health care the puppy is to receive once it leaves the breeder's facility. This typically includes details about the dog's current health and the recommendations for the next steps in the puppy's health care. Guarantees may also provide veterinary schedules to ensure the health care started by the breeder is continued by the new puppy parent. In the event that a major health concern surfaces, the puppy will be returned to the breeder.

The contract will also explain what is not covered by the guarantee. A guarantee tends to be quite long (sometimes longer than the contract), and you should also read it thoroughly before signing it.

Weimaraner contracts usually include a requirement that the dog is spayed or neutered once it reaches maturity (typically six months). The contract may also contain requirements for naming your puppy (if you would like more information about naming requirements, check out the American Kennel Club for details about contracts), details of the puppy's health, and a stipulation regarding what will happen if you can no longer take care of the animal. Information concerning the steps that will be taken if the new owner is negligent or abusive to the dog is also included in the contract.

Health Tests and Certifications

> *Get health certifications from breeders. The pups should be gray (not blue) and should leave at around eight weeks of age. The breeder should have a socializing plan for pups so that they are confident.*
>
> **ELENA LAMBERSON**
> *Silversmith Weimaraners*

A healthy puppy requires healthy parents and a clean genetic history, which is a bit more difficult to guarantee in a Weimaraner due to the history of this breed. A conscientious breeder keeps extensive records of each puppy and its parents. You should review each of the parents' complete histories to understand what traits your puppy is likely to inherit. Pay attention to temperament, learning traits, attachment issues, and any other personality traits you consider important. You can request these documents be sent to you electronically, or you can pick them up when you visit the breeder in person.

It might be time-consuming to review the breeder's information for each parent, but it is always well worth the time. The more you know about the parents, the better prepared you will be for your puppy.

There are a number of tests that must be run on Weimaraner parents to make sure the puppies are unlikely to have the known genetic issues associated with the breed:
- Genetic Testing for Hyperuricosuria, Hypomyelination, and Spinal Dysraphisim
- Hip Evaluation
- Autoimmune Thyroiditis
- Eye Certification
- Cardiac (Recommended)
- Elbow Dysplasia (Recommended)

These tests do not guarantee the puppies won't have problems, but parents who score well on the tests are less likely to pass on genetic issues. Chapter 17 details the health issues that are common to the breed, their symptoms, and potential treatments.

Selecting a Puppy from a Breeder

> *When choosing from a breeder, it is important to trust that the person is honest and knowledgeable about the breed. Choose a pup from proven hunting lines or working lines if you are wanting to hunt with the dog or do other competitive activities. If you are wanting a pet puppy, choose a pup from lines that are not as active.*
>
> ANNE TYSON
> *Regen Weimaraners*

Selecting your puppy should be done in person. However, if the breeder is willing to share videos and pictures, you can start checking out your puppy immediately after he is born!

Photo Courtesy of Dawna Miller

This is something to keep in mind as you check out the puppies. If you are looking for a more laid-back dog, the first one to greet you probably isn't going to be that dog. You should consider the following steps once you are allowed to visit the puppies in person:

- Assess the group of puppies as a whole. If most or all of the puppies are aggressive or fearful, this is an indication of a problem with the litter or (more likely) the breeder. The following are considered red flags if they are displayed by a majority of the puppies:
  - ☐ Tucked tails
  - ☐ Shrinking away from people
  - ☐ Whimpering when people get close
  - ☐ Constant attacking of your hands or feet (beyond pouncing)

- Notice how each puppy plays with the other puppies in the litter. This is a great indicator of how your puppy will react to any pets you already have at home. If you see problems with the way one puppy plays, this could be a problem later.

- Notice which puppies greet you first and which puppies hang back to observe you from afar. This lets you know their personality and how likely they are to be laid back later.

- Puppies should not be over or underweight. A swollen stomach is generally a sign of worms or other health problems.
- Puppies should have straight, sturdy legs. Splayed legs can be a sign there is something wrong.
- Examine the puppy's ears for mites, which will cause a discharge if present. The inside of the ear should be pink, not red or inflamed.
- The eyes should be clear and bright.
- Check the puppy's mouth for pink, healthy-looking gums.
- Pet the puppy to check his coat for the following:
  - Be sure the coat feels thick and full. If breeders have allowed puppies' fur to get matted or dirty, it is an indication they are probably not taking proper care of the animals.
  - Check for fleas and mites by running your hand from the head to the tail, then check under the tail, as fleas are more likely to hide there. If mites are present, they may look like dandruff.
- Check the puppy's rump for redness and sores; try to check the puppy's last bowel movement to ensure its firmness.

Pick the puppy that exhibits the personality traits you want in your dog. If you want a forward, friendly, excitable dog, the first puppy to greet you may be the one you choose. If you want a dog that will think things through and let others get more attention, look for a puppy that sits back and observes before approaching you. That initial reaction should be on the puppy's terms as much as your own so that you can determine if the personality matches what you think will fit best in your home.

CHAPTER 5

Preparing Your Budget and Family for Your New Weimaraner

Weimaraners can get quite expensive, depending on what kinds of activities you want to enjoy with your dog. Their size means they need more food, larger equipment, and sturdier and larger toys. The budget for the first year is going to be a lot higher for a Weimaraner than for a small or medium-sized dog because that cute little puppy is going to quickly outgrow everything you purchased for his arrival. You should be prepared to adjust crates, collars, and other equipment so that they aren't too small for your growing puppy. If you get an adult, this won't be a problem—you'll just need to buy the large equipment right from the start.

Part 3 of this book goes into the details of the training and socialization of your Weimaraner. If you plan to take your dog to classes, you will need to do some research into the costs in your specific area. Make sure to include that cost in your budget. Breeders tend to strongly recommend you plan on early classes because it can help your dog learn with some distractions, as well as give you someone who can help you during those difficult first sessions.

This chapter will provide the details for the majority of the costs that you will need to cover to ensure you have all of the items your new pup will need before he arrives and over the first year. Since you can go online and get all of these items, the cost is a lot more predictable.

Chapter 5: Preparing Your Budget and Family for Your New Weimaraner

The rest of this chapter details what you need to do to prepare your family for the dog's arrival. It is a very exciting time, so before your Weimaraner arrives, you want to make sure you have all your ducks in a row.

Planning the First Year's Budget

Whether you get a puppy or an adult dog, the costs are always higher than you initially thought. You will definitely want a budget, which is a good reason to start purchasing supplies a few months in advance. As you buy the items you need, you will begin to formulate an idea of how much money you will spend each month. Many of these items are one-time purchases (or won't need to be bought too often, like a bed), but many other items, like food and treats, will have to be purchased regularly.

The following table will help you plan your budget. Keep in mind the prices are rough estimates and may be significantly different based on your location.

Item	Considerations	Estimated Costs
Crate	You will need two crates—one for the puppy and one for when the puppy grows up. Even a puppy can weigh 36 lbs. at three months. This should be a comfortable space where the puppy will sleep and rest.	Wire crates: $60 to $350 Portable crate: $35 to $200
Bed	You will probably need two beds—one for the puppy and one for when the pup grows up. This will be placed in the crate.	$10 to $55
Leash	The leash should be short in the beginning because you need to be able to keep your puppy from getting overexcited and running to the end of a long line.	Short leash: $6 to $15 Retractable: $8 to $25
Doggie bags for walks	If you walk in parks, this won't be necessary. For those who don't have daily access to free doggy bags, it is best to purchase packs to ensure you don't run out.	Singles: less than $1 each. Packs: $4 to $16
Collar	You will need two collars—one for the puppy and one for an adult Weimaraner.	$10 to $30
Tags	These will probably be provided by your vet. Find out what information the vet provides for tags, then purchase any tags that are not provided. At a minimum, your Weimaraner should have a tag with your address on it in case the pup escapes.	Contact your vet before purchasing to see if the required rabies tags include your contact info.
Puppy food	This is going to depend on if you make your Weimaraner food, purchase food, or both. The larger the bag, the higher the cost, but the fewer times you will need to purchase food. You will need to purchase puppy-specific food in the beginning, but that will stop after the second year. Adult dog food is more expensive, particularly for large breeds like the Weimaraner.	$9 to $90 per bag

Chapter 5: Preparing Your Budget and Family for Your New Weimaraner

Item	Considerations	Estimated Costs
Water and food bowls	These will need to be kept in the puppy's area. If you have other dogs, you will need separate bowls for the puppy.	$10 to $40
Toothbrush/ Toothpaste	You will need to brush your dog's teeth regularly, so plan to use more than one toothbrush during the first year.	$2.50 to $14
Brush	Weimaraner coats are easy to maintain, and you should brush them regularly. When they are puppies, brushing offers a great way to bond.	$3.50 to $20
Toys	You definitely want to get your puppy toys for aggressive chewers. You will want to keep getting your Weimaraner toys as an adult (cost of adult dog toys not included).	$2.00 Packs of toys range from $10 to $20 (easier in the long run as your pup will chew through toys quickly)
Training treats	You will need these from the beginning and probably won't need to change the treats based on your dog's age; you may need to change treats to keep your dog's interest, though.	$4.50 to $15

You will need to pay attention to when items need to be replaced based on your dog's size. Ultimately, you need to establish a budget for the initial costs, then create a second budget for items that will need to be replaced. Plan to revisit this list at the end of every year for the first two years so you can make sure your dog remains comfortable and happy.

When you contact a vet to plan your first visit with your Weimaraner, request a cost estimate for that first year. The cost is substantially different for shots in a major city than in a rural area. Take the rough estimate for shots and other vet costs and add it to your budget planning for that first year. Also, put the date of the first vet visit on your calendar.

Finally, you will probably want to look up ways to clean, especially in areas where your dog eats and drinks. This is a very drooly, big dog that can leave slobber behind on walls. You may find yourself using extra napkins or paper towels. Consider getting a few cloths that you can keep near areas where your dog is likely to drool all over the walls or furniture so you can quickly clean it up.

Instructing Your Children

All large dogs need children around them to understand and abide by the rules of how to interact. This is true even with a puppy because the puppy needs to feel safe in the new home. You will need to be firm with children to make sure they don't accidentally hurt your Weimaraner or teach your new dog to be too hyperactive. As he gets bigger, your puppy can become a potential danger if he is reckless around your children.

To help your puppy feel comfortable in his new home, you must make sure your children are careful and gentle with the dog, whether a puppy or an adult. Some kids may try to treat the puppy like a toy; don't let them. Take the time to make sure your children follow all of the "puppy rules" from the very beginning to ensure your puppy feels safe, happy, and isn't accidentally injured.

The following are the Five Golden Rules your children should follow from day one. They apply both to puppies and adult Weimaraners:

1. Always be gentle and respectful.
2. Do not disturb the puppy during mealtimes.
3. Chase is an outside game.
4. The Weimaraner should always remain firmly on the ground. Never pick him up.
5. All valuables should be kept out of the puppy's reach.

Since your kids are going to ask why these rules are necessary, the following are some explanations you can use. If necessary, modify the discussion to meet the audience—what you say to a toddler is a lot different from what you should tell a teen about playing with your Weimaraner.

Weimaraners tend to love children. You do still need to monitor younger children until you know your dog won't become too excited. Younger children may get a little too rough, and no matter how sturdy

Chapter 5: Preparing Your Budget and Family for Your New Weimaraner

Weimaraners are, you don't want your new family member to get hurt by an overexcited child.

Always Be Gentle and Respectful

At no time should anyone be rough with a puppy. It is important to be respectful of your puppy to help him learn to also be respectful toward people and other animals.

This rule must be applied consistently every time your children play with your puppy. Be firm if you see your children getting too excited or rough. You don't want the puppy to get overly excited either because he might end up nipping or biting someone. If he does, it won't be his fault because he is still learning. Make sure your children understand the possible repercussions if they get too rough.

Mealtime

Weimaraners can be protective of their food, especially if you rescue a dog that has previously had to fend for himself. Even if you have a puppy, you don't want him to feel insecure during his mealtime because he will learn to be aggressive whenever he eats. Save yourself, your family, and your dog future problems by making sure mealtime is your dog's time alone. Teach your children their own mealtime is off-limits to the puppy, as well.

No feeding your new dog from the table! From toddlers

HELPFUL TIP

An Active Child's Best Friend

These high-energy, silver-coated dogs are known for their loyalty and can make excellent family dogs. However, because Weimaraners are exceptionally energetic, they'll need frequent exercise to avoid becoming too rambunctious around small children. When introducing a dog to young children, it's important to set healthy expectations and never leave children unattended with a dog. With plenty of exercise and responsible supervision, a Weimaraner could become your active child's new best friend.

to teens, this is something you'll really need to emphasize—particularly for foods that your kids don't like. Weimaraners are pets, not garbage disposals, and no amount of cute puppy eyes should be rewarded with scraps from the table. That is a recipe for disaster, as it will get harder to convince your dog to stop begging if other people aren't following your rules.

Photo Courtesy of Annabella Alfaro

Chase

Make sure your children understand why a game of chase may be all right outdoors (though you'll need to monitor things), but inside the house, chasing is off-limits! A three-month-old puppy is hard enough to control when he is excited and running inside the house, but a 90-pound, eight-month-old puppy will be nearly impossible to manage and can do a lot of damage inside.

Running inside your home gives your Weimaraner puppy the impression your home isn't safe for him because he is being chased; it also teaches your puppy that running indoors is allowed, which can be dangerous as the dog gets older and bigger. One of the last things you want to see is your adult Weimaraner go barreling through your home—knocking into people and furniture—because he learned it was fine for him to run in the house when he was a puppy!

Paws on the Ground

It doesn't matter how adorable your Weimaraner is—he is a living, breathing creature, and he needs to have his paws on the ground (even though he will quickly grow too big to pick up). You might want to carry your new family member around or play with the pup like a baby, but you and your family will have to resist that urge. The younger your children are, the more difficult it will be for them to understand the difference. It is so tempting to treat the puppy like a baby, but this is uncomfortable and unhealthy for the puppy.

Older children will quickly learn that a puppy's nip or bite hurts a lot more than one would think. Those little teeth are quite sharp, and if a dog nips, he could accidentally be dropped—no one wants that to happen. If your children are never allowed to pick up the puppy, things will be a lot better for everyone involved. Remember, this also applies to you, so don't make things difficult by doing something you constantly tell your children not to do.

Keep Valuables Out of Reach

> *As with any dog, a new owner will want to keep things out of the new dog's reach. Weimaraners can be destructive, especially when they are young, teething puppies. Acclimate the new Weim to the surrounding outside areas, as they are a breed that learns boundaries very well.*
>
> JOE WIDOMSKI
> *Shade of Grey Weimaraners*

Your kids will be less than happy if their personal possessions are chewed up by an inquisitive puppy, so teach them to put toys, clothes, and other valuables far out of the puppy's reach. Given how big your Weimaraner will get, you may need to get creative in how you get things out of reach. Cupboards, drawers, and other types of cabinets will probably be essential to ensuring your Weimaraner can't access things you don't want destroyed. Until they are a couple of years old, Weimaraners are far from mellow, and when left alone, destroying things will be their go-to activity when no one is around to entertain them.

Preparing Your Current Dogs and Cats

It can be a bit tricky introducing Weimaraners to a home with small animals and cats. Even puppies may want to chase those animals. To get the most well-rounded dog possible, you should start socializing him with your other dogs or pets when he is still a puppy. In most cases, this is a fairly straightforward process as long as your established pets are comfortable with you bringing a new puppy into their home. Even cats may find they can put up with your Weimaraner puppy as long as you can convince your new dog not to chase the cats. Given their history, this could prove to be a real challenge in the early days with your Weimaraner. Plan to have a safe space for your cats where your Weimaraner can't go so that your cats have somewhere they can feel safe from the exuberance of a puppy that wants nothing more than to chase them.

The following are important tasks you should complete when preparing your current pets for the new arrival:
- Set a schedule of activities and the people who will need to participate.
- Preserve your current dog's favorite places and furniture; make sure your current dog's toys and other personal items are not in the puppy's space.
- Have playdates at your home to observe your dog(s) reactions to having an addition to the house.

Stick to a Schedule

> *Weims do best with consistent boundaries and a regular routine.*
>
> ANNE TYSON
> *Regen Weimaraners*

It's essential to have a schedule. Obviously, the puppy is going to receive a lot of attention in the beginning, so you need to make a concerted effort to be sure your current pet(s) know you will still care for them. Set a specific time in your schedule when you can show your current dog(s) how much you love him (them), and make sure you don't stray from that schedule after the puppy arrives.

When you bring the puppy home, plan to have at least one adult present for each dog you have in your home. If you have a cat in the home, the introduction will need to be slow and methodical. If you bring home an adult Weimaraner, you will need to be careful and keep the dog and cat separated when you aren't around to monitor them because Weimaraners have a high prey drive. Over time, it is likely they will learn to be fine with each other. Weimaraners may have difficulty getting along with other dogs of the same gender, so ask about this if you are bringing home an adult Weimaraner.

Photo Courtesy of Terry Clark

Having a schedule in place for your other dogs will make it easier to follow the plan with the puppy. Once he has arrived, your puppy is going to eat, sleep, and spend most of the day and night in his assigned space. This means your puppy's space cannot block your current canine's favorite furniture, bed, or anywhere he rests during the day. None of your current dog's "stuff" should be in the puppy's area either; this includes toys. You don't want your older dog to feel as if the puppy is taking over his territory. Make sure your children also understand to never put your current dog's things in the puppy's area!

Your dog and your puppy will need to be kept apart at the beginning (even if they seem friendly) until your puppy has received all of his vaccinations. Puppies are more susceptible to illness during these early days, so wait until the puppy is protected from possible diseases before the dogs spend time together. Leaving the puppy in his puppy space will keep the dogs separated during this critical time.

Helping Your Dog Prepare — Extra at-Home Playdates

The following explains strategies that will help prepare your current pooch for the arrival of your puppy:

- Consider the personality of your dog to predict what might happen when the puppy arrives. If your current dog loves other dogs, this will probably hold true when the puppy shows up. If your current dog is territorial, you will need to be cautious when introducing the two dogs, at least until the Weimaraner has become part of the pack. Excitable dogs need special attention to keep them from getting agitated when a new dog comes home. You don't want your current dog to be so excited that he makes the Weimaraner feel threatened.
- Consider the times when unfamiliar dogs have been in your home. How did your current dog react to these other furry visitors? If your canine becomes territorial, be cautious when introducing your new pup. If you have never invited another dog into your home, organize a playdate with other dogs before your Weimaraner puppy arrives. You need to know how your current furry babies will react to new dogs in the house so that you can properly prepare. Meeting a dog at home is quite different from encountering one outside the home.
- Think about your established dog's interactions with other dogs for as long as you have known him. Has your dog shown protective or possessive behavior, either with you or others? Food is one of the reasons dogs will display aggression because they don't want anyone eating what is theirs. Some dogs can be protective of people and toys too.
- If you know someone who owns a Weimaraner, organize a playdate so that your current dog becomes aware of the temperament of a Weimaraner.

These same rules apply no matter how many dogs you have. Think about their individual personalities as well as how they interact together.

Chapter 5: Preparing Your Budget and Family for Your New Weimaraner

Photo Courtesy of Lisa Shriver

Similar to humans, you may find when your dogs are together, they act differently. This is something you will need to keep in mind as you plan their first introduction. (Details of how to introduce your current dog(s) and your new puppy—plus how to juggle the two new personalities—are included in Chapter 9.)

CHAPTER 6

Preparing Your Home and Schedule

The amount of time you need to spend preparing your home for a puppy versus an adult is about the same, but what you have to do is going to be very different, especially with a large dog. With a puppy, you are essentially going to need to childproof your home for toddlers. With an adult, you are going to need to kid-proof it for a large child, and you should have gates to keep your dog contained to certain areas as you figure out how he will interact with the surroundings. Doors may be enough, but you'll want gates and a dedicated area for both puppies and adults. This is an intelligent dog that can figure things out, so if you have doors that have handles instead of knobs (especially those that pull down), he may be able to figure out how to get out of a room with a door. For an intelligent, curious dog like the Weimaraner, you even need to childproof cabinets and areas that you wouldn't need to with a puppy, at least until your dog knows and understands the rules.

Puppy-proofing a home is nearly identical to childproofing it, but you are going to have to secure areas that are much higher up since the Weimaraner puppy is going to grow quickly. Coupled with problem-solving skills, your Weimaraner is going to be able to get into things that he really shouldn't, with food left on kitchen countertops being at particularly high risk. Protecting your Weimaraner is the priority. You need to make sure the dog isn't able to get out of the yard or make his way into rooms that are potentially dangerous for him.

You need to complete these efforts several weeks before your dog is planned to arrive. Then you should conduct a weekly review leading up to your Weimaraner's arrival to make sure you don't miss anything and that everything is in place. You will need to check higher areas for an adult

Chapter 6: Preparing Your Home and Schedule

Photo Courtesy of Annabella Alfaro

Weimaraner than for smaller dogs, especially when it comes to cords and other chewable things that could harm your dog. Your new family member should have a safe space that includes all of the essentials. This will help to make your dog more comfortable and make the initial arrival a great experience for everyone.

As an intelligent breed, the Weimaraner has to know that you are the leader to follow and listen to, so you will need to earn your new family member's respect, which is easier with a puppy than it is with an adult (though it is easier to make exceptions for a puppy over an adult, which you should not do). This is why it is absolutely essential to ensure you are firm and consistent when you are training and working with your

Weimaraner. When he understands you mean what you say, that will go a long way to letting him know why he should listen to you.

Before diving into everything you need to do, here's what one breeder had to say about what needs to be done prior to your new dog's arrival:

> *A secure yard is paramount to the growing and mature Weimaraner's safety. It should be completely fenced, with no avenues for escape. Like a toddler, your dog will find them! Originally bred in European countries for hunting large and small game—think deer, wild boars, wolves, foxes, rabbits, and birds—Weimaraners will dig under fences and jump over fences if they want to get at something bad enough; unfortunately, this also can include squirrels and cats. Some dogs can easily dig 1-2 feet and jump 5-6 feet.*
>
> *Obviously, a hole in the barrier is an open door for trouble and must be secured. Let me also mention that while invisible/electric fences can be utilized with very well-trained dogs, they do not prevent animals from entering your yard, and some Weimaraners will choose to take the shock to get at their desired prey. They are doing what they were bred to do; consistent training is paramount.*
>
> **KYRA SCHLIEMAN,**
> *SilverLining Weimaraners*

Creating a Safe Space for Your Adult Dog or Puppy

Your new dog will need a dedicated space that includes a crate, food and water bowls, pee pads, and toys. All of these things should be in the area where the puppy will stay when you are not able to give him attention. The puppy's space should be gated so that your Weimaraner cannot get out and young children (or dogs) cannot get in. It should be a safe space where the puppy can see you going about your usual business and feel comfortable.

An adult Weimaraner will need a similar setup as a puppy, with all of the same items, but you can give the adult dog a bigger area. Pee pads may be necessary while the adult dog adjusts to the new environment, even if the dog is already house-trained.

Crates — An Absolute Essential for Weimaraners

> *A crate is the best training aid! Take your out pup when it first wakes up and after meals. Don't leave the puppy unattended when it is loose!*
>
> **CHRISTINE GRISELL**
> *Nani's Weimaraners*

Crate training (discussed in detail in Chapter 7) is much more likely to be difficult if you have a crate that is too big, too small, or too uncomfortable for your dog to feel like it is a safe place. To make training easier, be sure the crate and bedding are set up and ready before your dog arrives. A small, cozy space will help your dog feel comfortable while also dissuading him from using it as a restroom since he won't be able to get away from any mess he makes. If you feed your dog in the crate, he will start to associate the crate with positive things. This is a dog that can be easily swayed by food, so this is one way to help your Weimaraner think of his crate as a place he wants to be.

Never treat the crate like it is a prison for your puppy or adult dog. It's meant to be a safe haven after overstimulation or a comfortable place to go when it's time to sleep. Ensure your dog never associates the crate with punishment or negative emotions. You can also get your puppy a carrying crate in the early days to make trips to the vet easier.

Both puppies and adult dogs are going to spend a good bit of time in the crate in those early days, though adults will be able to roam your home a lot faster. At least, if the adult is already house-trained, it will be a much faster process to get away from the crate.

Puppy-Proof/Dog-Proof the House

The most dangerous rooms and items in your home will be as dangerous to your puppy as if he were a little baby. The biggest difference is your Weimaraner is going to become mobile much faster than a child. He will get into dangerous situations immediately if you don't eliminate all the hazards before his arrival. Be aware that puppies will try to eat virtually anything! Nothing is safe—not even your furniture—and they will also gnaw on wood and metal or clothing. Anything within reach is considered fair game! This is true for adult dogs too, but clearly, their reach will be a lot higher off the ground, including in your kitchen.

Keep this in mind as you go about dog-proofing your home. You will need to look for dangers and make sure they are removed before your Weimaraner arrives, whether he is a puppy or an adult.

> **HELPFUL TIP**
> **Mischief Makers**
>
> Weimaraners are exceptionally smart dogs, often ranked between the 20th and 25th most intelligent breeds. However, this canine brainpower may require extra puppy-proofing in your home. For example, some Weimaraner owners report witnessing their dogs opening refrigerator doors and climbing fences when unattended. Therefore, baby locks on food cabinets and refrigerators may be necessary for particularly exploratory dogs, and fences should be at least five feet tall to prevent escape efforts.

Plant Dangers

Plants pose a unique risk to dogs because we are less likely to consider them than we might with a toddler or small child. Pets have a much greater tendency to try to eat plants, so you have to learn about all of the greenery around your home to make sure your Weimaraner

Chapter 6: Preparing Your Home and Schedule

doesn't try to supplement the food you give him with something that is potentially hazardous to his health.

Remember to check both inside and outside your home.

Mildly Toxic	Mildly to Moderately Toxic	Moderately Toxic	Moderately to Highly Toxic	Highly Toxic
Asparagus Fern	Aloe	Alocasia	Cactus	Brunfelsia
Begonia	Amaryllis	Arrowhead	Kalanchoe	Desert Rose
Ficus Benjamina	Calla Lily	Dieffenbachia		Flame Lily
Flamingo Flower	Cyclamen	Dracaena Fragrans		Kaffir Lily
Gardenia	Dracaena	English Ivy		Oleander
Geranium	Philodendron	Eucalyptus		Sago Palm
Golden Pothos		Peyote		Bird of Paradise (Strelitzia)
Jade Plant				
Schefflera				
Ti Plant				
ZZ Plant				

Photo Courtesy of Stacey Perez

Indoor Hazards and Fixes

> *They can break out of crates, jump over baby barriers, and unlock pantry doors. They love to dig, and they can jump! Make sure that the backyard fence is totally secure. That means a fence higher than five feet and buried partially to prevent digging underneath. Crate training is a must for indoor sanity, if you don't want the drywall eaten while you are out to dinner.*
>
> **TONI FOW**
> *Wing It Weimaraners*

Chapter 6: Preparing Your Home and Schedule

A Weimaraner will be an avid explorer, wanting to get into everything if given the opportunity, at least until he reaches a more mellow age. Get on your hands and knees to view each room from your Weimaraner's perspective prior to the dog's arrival. Even if they are a big breed, Weimaraners are clever and can get into areas you don't think they should be able to.

Hazards	Fixes	Time Estimate
Kitchen		
Poisons	Keep in secure, childproof cabinets or on high shelves.	30 min.
Trash Cans	Use a lockable trash can or keep it in a secure location.	10 min.
Appliances	Make sure all cords are out of reach.	15 min.
Human Food	Keep out of reach.	Constant (Start making it a habit!)
Floors		
Slippery Surfaces	Put down rugs or special mats designed to stick to the floor.	30 min. – 1 hour
Training Area	Train your Weimaraner on nonslip surfaces.	Constant
Bathrooms		
Toilet Brush	Either have one that locks into the container or keep the brush out of reach.	5 min.
Poisons	Keep in secure, childproof cabinets or on high shelves.	15–30 min.
Toilets	Keep lids closed.	
Do not use automatic toilet-cleaning chemicals.	Constant (Start making it a habit!)	
Cabinets	Keep secured with childproof locks.	15–30 min.

Hazards	Fixes	Time Estimate
Laundry Room		
Clothing	Store both clean and dirty clothes off the floor and out of reach.	15–30 min.
Poisons (bleach, pods/detergent, dryer sheets, and misc. poisons)	Keep in secure, childproof cabinets or on high shelves.	15 min.
Around the Home		
Plants	Keep off the floor.	45 min. – 1 hour
Trash Cans	Have a lockable trash can or keep it in a secure location.	10–30 min.
Electrical Cords/Window Blind Cords	Hide cords or make sure they are out of reach; pay particular attention to entertainment and computer areas.	1–1.5 hours
Poisons	Check to make sure there aren't any poisons in reach (WD40, window/screen cleaner, carpet cleaner, air fresheners); move all poisons to a central, locked location.	1 hour
Windows	Be sure cords are out of reach in all rooms.	1–2 hours
Fireplaces	Store cleaning supplies and tools where the dog can't get into them. Cover the fireplace opening with something the dog can't knock over.	10 min.
Stairs	Cordon off so that your puppy can't go up or down the stairs; make sure to test all puppy gates for safety.	10–15 min.
Coffee Tables/End Tables/Nightstands	Clear of dangerous objects (e.g., scissors, sewing equipment, pens, and pencils) and all valuables.	30–45 min.

If you have a cat, keep the litter box off the floor. It needs to be somewhere that your cat can easily get to it, but your Weimaraner cannot. Since this involves training your cat, it's something you should do well in advance of the dog's arrival. You don't want your cat to undergo too

Chapter 6: Preparing Your Home and Schedule

Photo Courtesy of Jeff Daugherty

many significant changes all at once. The new canine in the house will be enough of a disruption! If your cat associates the change with your Weimaraner, you may find the feline refusing to use the litter box.

To get the litter box out of your dog's reach, you'll need to put it up high and preferably with several levels to allow your cat to reach it, but where it will be out of reach of your very large dog. It won't be long before your puppy will be able to get into a litter box on a cabinet, so you need to find a place accessible to cats but not to massive dogs.

Finally, in case of problems, be sure your vet's number is posted on the fridge and in at least one other room in the house. Even if the number is programmed into your phone, family members or dog sitters will still need to know who to call.

Outdoor Hazards and Fixes

The area outside your home also needs dog-proofing. As with the inside, you will need to check your outdoor preparations by getting down low and inspecting all areas from a puppy's perspective. Remember to also post the vet's number in one of the sheltered outdoor areas in case of an emergency.

Hazards	Fixes	Time Estimate
Garage		
Poisons	Keep in secure, childproof cabinets or on high shelves (e.g., car chemicals, cleaning supplies, paint, lawn care)—this includes fertilizer.	1 hour
Trash Bins	Keep them in a secure location.	5 min.
Tools (e.g., lawn, car, hardware, power tools)	Make sure all cords are kept out of reach and never hang over the side of surfaces.	30 min. - 1 hour
Equipment (e.g., sports, fishing)	Keep out of reach, and never allow them to hang over the side of surfaces.	Constant (Start making it a habit!)
Sharp Implements	Keep out of reach, and never allow them to hang over the side of surfaces.	30 min.
Bikes	Store off the ground or in a place the Weimaraner cannot get to (to keep the pup from biting the tires).	20 min.
Fencing (Can Be Done Concurrently)		
Breaks	Fix any breaks in the fencing. You need to make sure your Weimaraner can't easily get out of your yard.	30 min. - 1 hour
Gaps	Fill in any gaps so that your Weimaraner doesn't escape.	30 min. - 1 hour
Holes/Dips at Base	Fill in any area that can be easily crawled under.	1-2 hours
Yard		
Poisons	Don't leave any poisons in the yard.	1-2 hours
Plants	Verify that low plants aren't poisonous; fence off anything that is (such as grapevines).	45 min. - 1 hour

If you have a pool, make sure it is secure so that your dog cannot get into it without your help. Covers may not always be enough, so make sure to have fencing or some other kind of deterrent to keep your Weimaraner safe. Even if your dog loves swimming, make sure you are always around when he is in the pool. Weimaraners tend to be excellent swimmers, but that doesn't mean they know when they've hit their limits. This isn't a dog that is known for quitting after getting hurt or understanding when it is too exhausted to keep going. Weimaraners want to be engaged and active, so you have to be the one to make sure they don't overexert themselves.

Never leave your Weimaraner alone in the garage, even when the dog is an adult. Your puppy may be in the garage when you take car trips, which is why it is important to puppy-proof this area. An adult can get into even more trouble, which is pretty much inevitable when he gets bored.

Make room in your schedule for monthly inspections because Weimaraners may dig out of boredom or could damage a fence as a form of entertainment. This is also why you can never leave your Weimaraner alone outside. Always attend to your dog when he goes out to the bathroom or to play because when he is bored, he will very likely start to create ways to get out of the yard. You don't want to put your dog out to use the bathroom only to find he has escaped in the five minutes you left him outside alone.

Some dogs have even been able to break through or knock over fences because they want to hang out with the people on the other side of the fence. Even chain-link fences aren't entirely a deterrent because this is a dog that is both smart enough and athletic enough to be able to climb out. It's quite a sight to watch them figure this out.

Choosing Your Veterinarian

You should choose a vet before you bring your dog home because scheduling a veterinary appointment may take a while. Unfortunately, you may not find a vet who has experience with the breed. Try to find a vet that at least has some experience with bigger work dogs.

Photo Courtesy of Sandra Sapatka

Every dog, regardless of age, should see a vet within the first 48 hours of its arrival home. The point is to establish your dog's baseline health. This may also be a requirement included in the contract with the breeder. Twenty-four hours is strongly recommended to make sure your dog is healthy, but this may not always be possible, which is why many places say to have it done within 48 hours. If there is a vet near you who specializes in or has worked with Weimaraners before, that will be best for your pup.

The following are some things to consider when looking for a vet:

What is the vet's level of familiarity with Weimaraners or similar dogs, like Dalmatians and Pointers?

It is almost guaranteed that vets in your area will not have experience with the breed, but experience with bigger work dogs is usually helpful in learning how to treat a Weimaraner. It is far more likely that vets have experience with Bulldogs, so you can ask about the vet's experience with them as well.

- How far from your home is the vet? (You don't want the vet to be more than 30 minutes away in case of an emergency.)
- Is the vet available for emergencies after hours, or can they recommend a vet in case of an emergency?
- Is the vet part of a local veterinary hospital, or does the vet refer patients to a local pet hospital?
- Is the vet one of several partners, or do they work alone? If the vet belongs to a partnership, can your dog see the same vet for all office visits?
- How are appointments booked?
- Can other services be performed at the clinic, such as grooming and boarding?
- Is the vet accredited?
- What is the price for the initial visit? What are the costs for routine visits that might include such things as shots?
- What tests and checks are performed during the initial visit?
- Can you visit the vet you are considering before you bring your dog home?

If so, inspect the office environment and ask if you can speak to the vet. The vet should be willing to put you at ease and answer your questions. Even though a vet's time is valuable, they should take a few minutes to help you feel confident about your decision to trust them with your new dog's health.

CHAPTER 7

Bringing Your Weimaraner Home

Weimaraners wear their emotions on their sleeves, and that will make the arrival of your new Weimaraner incredibly memorable. It's impossible to guess just how your dog will react, but you'll be able to guess how your dog is feeling with ease. Your canine will

Photo Courtesy of April Tyler

almost certainly have a sense of apprehension about a new place with all new people, but there will also be a sense of excitement for something new. By working to make it a happy, fun, and safe experience, you can make a great first impression on your newest family member.

Although this is a breed that is prone to being quite friendly, new situations are going to be scary for him. That's why you want to make your Weimaraner as comfortable as possible, to let him know that your home is a safe environment. This chapter covers how to introduce your new Weimaraner to your home in a way that establishes a sense of safety so that he can settle in quicker. If you already have a dog, refer to Chapter 8 because you will need to introduce the animals outside of the home before your pup makes his grand entrance. Once you understand how to introduce dogs to each other, come back to this chapter to learn how to introduce your new family member to your home and any family members who weren't able to make the initial meet and greet.

If you don't have dogs, read ahead to see what to expect and how to make the experience more enjoyable for your Weimaraner.

Final Preparations and Planning

If you are bringing home a puppy, there are good odds that there will be a lot of anxiety and nervousness on his part. Adult dogs are less likely to feel this way unless they were at their previous home long enough to get comfortable (this is usually not the case at shelters or similar rescues), but they will still feel some level of anxiety and be wary in their new surroundings.

You can try to minimize the negative emotions, starting with taking time off from work during the first 24 to 48 hours after your dog comes home; the best-case scenario would have you at home for the first week or two. The more time you dedicate to helping your new friend become accustomed to his surroundings, the better. It's similar to taking time off when you bring home a baby. The focus is on bonding and establishing a good relationship with your dog.

Ensure You Have Food and Other Supplies on Hand

The day before your Weimaraner arrives, review the list in Chapter 5 and do a quick check to ensure you have everything you need. Take a few moments to consider if there is anything you are missing. This will keep you from having to rush out for additional supplies after the arrival of your new family member.

If you plan to make your dog's food, make sure you have the supplies and extra time in your schedule. Keep it all in one place so that you don't have to spend time hunting for the supplies when it's time to eat.

One breeder very succinctly explained what you are in for once your dog arrives:

> *A Weim pup is like a two-year-old toddler. They will get into everything. If you are not able to watch him, put him in a crate. Take him outside frequently. Leash train from day one. Pup will get into plants, closets, electric cords, trash cans, etc. Be prepared!*
>
> **ELENA LAMBERSON**
> *Silversmith Weimaraners*

Use this reminder to make sure everything is in place before that bundle of energy reaches your door.

Design a Tentative Puppy Schedule

> *Puppies need a schedule and structure. The first night with a puppy sleeping in a crate can be stressful. Don't give up! Crate the pup close to the owners' sleeping quarters/next to the bed, and comfort it if it is having trouble settling. Just your voice can be enough to let the puppy know you're close by. Puppies typically settle into your routine in a couple of nights. Also, crate the puppy when you're home. Don't let it associate the crate with you leaving. Let it see the crate as a safe place.*
>
> **CAMILLE RICE**
> *Timberdoodle Weimaraners*

Weimaraners require a firm hand to keep them from misusing all of their energy, and a schedule can establish that you are the one dictating how things will go while giving them something to learn. It won't take long before your Weimaraner starts to put together when to expect a meal or trip outside. They are a very intelligent breed, so once they put this together (perhaps with a treat or a bit of extra playtime after

FUN FACT
Puppy Stripes

Adult Weimaraner's coats are iconically silver gray, but puppies of this breed have an exciting, albeit short-lived trait. Weimaraner puppies are born with dark gray "tiger stripes" on a light gray background. However, these stripes fade away within the first few days of the puppy's life.

they potty), they will be taking you to the door after they finish eating. You will need to be consistent in the beginning, but it will get increasingly easy to do since your dog will be more than happy to remind you of the schedule once he learns it.

Prepare a tentative schedule to help you get started over the course of the first week. Your days are about to get remarkably busy, so you need somewhere to begin before your puppy arrives. As you settle into a routine, you can update the schedule since it isn't set in stone. Consider it more of a guideline so that you don't forget important tasks, especially taking your dog out for regular restroom breaks.

The following are three key areas to establish in the schedule before your puppy arrives:
- Feeding
- Training (including house-training)
- Playing

When you bring home a puppy, you may be expecting a ball of high energy. However, puppies of any breed (no matter how active they will be later) sleep between 18 and 20 hours per day. Having a predictable sleep schedule will help your puppy grow up to be healthier. Plan eating times, bathroom breaks, and playtime around your puppy's sleep schedule.

In the beginning, you won't need to worry about making sure that your puppy is tired out by the end of the day. Your puppy's schedule will revolve around sleeping and eating, with some walking and socialization time. His stamina will build fairly quickly, though; by the end of the first year, your pup will be a lot more active! As your pup starts to sleep less and play more, he will need 30 to 60 minutes of daily physical activity.

Every puppy is different, even within a single breed, so adjust the schedule based on the changes you see with your dog.

Keep in mind this is a dog that was born and bred for hunting, and that is a very structured activity. The best way to ensure your dog starts to feel comfortable and understands what to expect is to give him a predictable life.

The next few sections will demonstrate why it is critical in the early days to establish a schedule; all puppies need a schedule, but with an intelligent, high-energy dog like the Weimaraner, a schedule can save your sanity in those early days.

Do a Quick Final Puppy-Readiness Inspection Before the Puppy Arrives

No matter how busy you are or how carefully you follow the puppy-proofing checklist, the day before your puppy arrives, be sure to set aside an hour or two to double-check that everything is in place. By giving it one final review before your dog arrives, you still have time to make last-minute changes or fixes before your dog is there.

Initial Meeting

Review the rules in Chapter 5 with all family members on the day of the dog's arrival and before the pup actually arrives. Place heavy emphasis on how to handle the Weimaraner, particularly the part about not picking up your newest family member. The puppy is already going to be in a state of shock, so don't compound that by literally taking the world out from under your Weimaraner's feet. Reinforce the rules with your children before the puppy arrives. Your children will be excited, perhaps as much as your new dog. From the first day, your children need to be on their best behavior so that your dog feels safe. Remember, following the rules goes both ways between your dog and your children.

Keep in mind that Weimaraners tend to be wary of strangers. Everyone needs to be aware to let the dog start interactions; people should not be screaming, squealing, or being otherwise very noisy, as this can be a source of anxiety for the Weimaraner. Also, people should not crowd around the puppy.

Determine who is going to be responsible for the primary puppy care and for primary training. To teach younger children responsibility, a parent can pair with a child to manage the puppy's care. The child can be responsible for feeding the puppy and keeping the water bowl filled. Of course, a parent should oversee these tasks.

Picking up Your Puppy or Dog and the Ride Home

> *Drive conservatively with a young puppy. Try not to make quick turns or stops/take-offs. Use slower speeds. It's disorienting for them and can contribute to motion sickness. Just as seat belts prevent injury in humans, dogs should be crated or secured with a safety harness when in a car for their safety in case of an accident.*
>
> **KYRA SCHLIEMAN**
> *SilverLining Weimaraners*

A good bit of planning and preparation goes into picking up your puppy, especially if you are going to the breeder's home. If possible, do this on a weekend or during a holiday season. This will allow you unrushed quality time at home with your new puppy.

As tempting as it is to cuddle the puppy in your lap, it is safer and more comfortable for the puppy if you use a crate for the ride home; two adults should also be present for the ride. This is the time to start teaching your puppy that car trips are enjoyable. This means making sure that the crate is securely anchored; you don't want the crate to slide around while the puppy is helplessly sitting inside it.

- The crate should be anchored in the car for safety and should include a cushion. If you have a long trip, bring food and water

Chapter 7: Bringing Your Weimaraner Home

Photo Courtesy of Michael Bill

for the puppy and plan to stop at regular intervals. Do not put food and water in the crate; sloshing water can scare your puppy. You can cover the bottom of the crate with a towel or pee pad in case of accidents.

- Call the breeder before you start the trip to make sure everything is still on schedule.
- Arrange for the mother dog to leave her scent on a blanket to help make the puppy's transition more comfortable.
- Make sure the second adult who will be traveling with you (highly recommended) will be on time so that the two of you can head to the pick-up destination.
- If you have other dogs, make sure all of the adults involved in the introduction process know what to do. They should know the time and place for that first neutral territory meeting.

If you do not have other dogs, you can pick up your puppy and head straight home. If you have a trip that lasts more than a couple of hours, stop periodically so your puppy can stretch, exercise, drink, and use the bathroom. Keep your puppy away from other dogs until he has gotten all of his shots; you don't want him to be exposed to a dog that is carrying a disease that your puppy is not fully protected against.

At no point should your puppy be left alone in the car. If you have to use the restroom, either go before leaving the breeder's place, or if you have a long drive ahead of you, have at least one adult remain with the puppy during each stop.

If the puppy has never ridden in a car before, someone should give him attention while the other person drives. The puppy should be in the crate, but someone can still provide comfort. The puppy will definitely be scared without his mom, siblings, or familiar people to console him. Having someone talk to the puppy will make it less of an ordeal for the little one.

When you arrive home, immediately take the puppy outside to use the bathroom. Even if he had an accident in his crate, this is the time to start training your new family member on where to use the bathroom.

The First Vet Visit and What to Expect

> *Crate in the car from a young age. Take your new puppy for rides, but in a crate! Be patient and make it fun. Just be silent if the puppy howls. The reward is when it gets to a fun place, not the vet!*
>
> **TONI FOW**
> *Wing It Weimaraners*

The first vet visit will establish a baseline for the puppy's health. This will also allow the vet to track your puppy's progress and monitor his health as he grows. In addition to providing a chance to ask questions and get advice, this initial assessment will give you more information

Chapter 7: Bringing Your Weimaraner Home

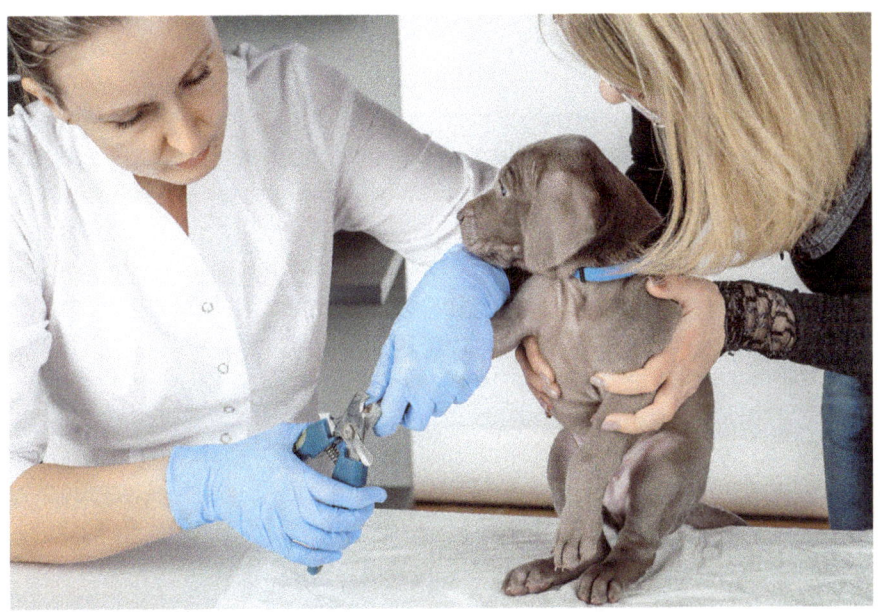

about your puppy. It also creates an important rapport between your Weimaraner and the vet.

During the first veterinary visit, your pup won't know what to expect. Try to ease his anxiety; you want this first appointment to set a positive tone for all future visits. This will likely be trickier with an adult dog than with a puppy, so be prepared to soothe any nervousness.

The following is a list of several things that must be completed before the day of the appointment:

- Find out how early you need to arrive to complete the paperwork for the new patient.
- Find out if you should bring a stool sample for that first visit. If so, collect it the morning of the visit and make sure to take it with you.
- Bring the paperwork provided by the breeder or rescue organization for the vet to add to your dog's records.

Your Weimaraner may want to meet the other pups and people in the office and will probably loudly announce your arrival. Although you will need to be mindful, this is an opportunity to socialize the puppy and to create a positive experience with the vet. Before letting your puppy meet other animals, always ask the owner for permission and wait for approval. Most pets at the vet's office are likely to not be feeling well, which means they may not be very affable. You don't want a grumpy older dog or a sick animal to nip or scare your puppy. Negative social experiences are situations your puppy will remember; they could make future visits to the vet something to dread. Nor do you want your puppy to be exposed to potential illnesses before he has had all of his shots.

Every vet is different, so you should call your vet ahead of your first visit to get an idea of everything that will be done. Odds are, you will need to bring documentation about your dog, so get your paperwork together when you go to the vet the first time.

Young puppies will need a series of shots. The vet may also request that you bring your dog's latest poop to check it for parasites. Chapter 16 provides more details on what to expect if parasites are detected in your dog's bowel movement.

Be prepared for the vet to ask about your dog's history, even though you just brought the Weimaraner home with you.

During the first visit, the vet will conduct an initial assessment of your Weimaraner. One of the most important things the vet will do is weigh your dog. This is something you are going to have to monitor for your dog's entire life, as you will want to ensure that your Weimaraner remains at a healthy weight. Keep a record of his weight so you can see how quickly your puppy is growing and to make sure you aren't overfeeding or underfeeding him. Ask your vet what is considered a healthy weight for every growth stage and record that as well.

The vet will set a date for the next group of shots, which will likely happen not too long after the initial visit. After your Weimaraner receives his vaccinations (detailed in Chapter 16), prepare for a couple of days of your puppy feeling under the weather.

The following are other checks the vet may make during that initial visit.

- Most vets will listen to your dog's heart and lungs to make sure there aren't any obvious problems.

- They will take your pup's temperature, so be prepared to help by calming your dog, as he's probably not going to be happy with this activity.
- Vets usually check a dog's ears, eyes, nose, paws, skin/coat, and genitals.
- They will do a longer check on the mouth and teeth to look for potential problems.
- They will do an initial check on the abdomen and lymph nodes.

If the vet does find a problem and recommends medication, take the time to ask questions and make sure you know what to do before you leave the office.

Crate and Other Preliminary Training

Contrary to what some people think, crates are a safe space for dogs. Crate training will also prepare your dog for occasions when you may have to board him, and he will be put in a crate if you ever travel on a plane.

With a dog like the Weimaraner, there are a few things you can do to make him associate the crate with positivity and security.

> *Introduce the puppy to the new surroundings and put toys and a couple of treats in the crate. Play with the puppy until he is tired and then introduce the crate to him when he wants a nap. Do not let him rest anywhere but the crate for the first couple of weeks.*
>
> **CHRISTINE GRISSELL**
> *Nani's Weimaraners*

Puppies younger than six months should not be left in a crate for hours at a time. Your Weimaraner will not be able to hold his bladder for very long, so you must make sure he has a way to get out and go to the bathroom. If you adopt an adult Weimaraner that is not house-trained, you will need to follow the same rules. If you aren't sure about whether or not the dog is house-trained, it is best to treat the adult as a puppy until you are certain that your newest family member won't use the house as a bathroom.

Make sure the crate door is set so that it doesn't close during your dog's initial sniff of the crate. You do not want your Weimaraner to be scared by the door as it is closing behind him; this could make him fearful of the crate in the future.

The following are some suggestions:
- Use a positive, cheerful voice as you let your Weimaraner sniff the crate for the first time. The first experience in the crate should be associated with excitement and positive emotions. Be sure your dog understands the crate is a good place. If you have a blanket from the puppy's mother, put it in the crate to help provide an extra sense of comfort.
- Drop a couple of treats into the crate if your canine seems reluctant to enter. Do NOT force your dog into the crate. If your dog refuses to go all the way inside the crate, that is perfectly fine. It has to be the dog's decision to enter so that it doesn't become a negative experience.
- Add a toy or two to indicate that the crate is a fun space. These can double for teething toys if you get a puppy—he will need those kinds of toys soon enough, and you want him chewing toys instead of your furniture or nibbling on you.
- For a week or two, feed your dog while he is in the crate. Besides keeping the food away from any other pets, this will create positive associations between your Weimaraner and the crate.
    - ☐ If your dog appears comfortable with the crate, put the food all the way at the back.
    - ☐ If not, place the food bowl in the front, then move it further back in the crate over time.
- Start closing the door once your dog appears to be eating comfortably in the crate. When the food is gone, open the crate door immediately.

Chapter 7: Bringing Your Weimaraner Home

- Leave the door closed for longer periods of time after your dog has finished eating. If your pup begins to whine, you know you have left your Weimaraner in the crate for too long.
- Crate your dog for longer periods of time once the dog shows no signs of discomfort while in the crate when eating. Train your Weimaraner to go into the crate by simply saying, "crate" or "bed." Then praise your dog to let him know that he has done an excellent job.

Repeat these steps for several weeks until your dog seems comfortable in the crate. The regular repetition several times a day teaches your dog that the crate is not a punishment and everything is all right. Initially, you should do this while you are still at home or when you go out to get the mail. When you leave the room and your puppy lasts half an hour without whining, you can leave the dog alone for longer periods of time. However, keep this alone time to no more than an hour in the beginning.

During the first few weeks, you should also begin to house-train your Weimaraner. Basic behavioral training is also vital from the start. However, wait until your Weimaraner has all of his vaccinations before taking him to structured training classes. Knowledgeable trainers will not accept puppies in their classes until a dog's first full round of shots is complete.

Apart from these initial types of training, you shouldn't be focused on training over the first week. That week should be for bonding. There will be plenty of time for training starting the second week.

Chapters 10 and 11 provide a closer look at how to train your dog.

First-Night Frights

That first night is going to be terrifying for your little Weimaraner puppy! As understandable as this may be, there is only so much comfort you can give your new family member. The more you respond to his cries and whimpering, the more he will learn negative behavior provides the desired results. You need to prepare for a balancing act—one that reassures the Weimaraner that he is safe while keeping him from associating crying with receiving attention from you.

This will be a tough time for your new dog, so here are some recommendations from a couple of breeders.

> *They will miss their mom and litter mates. Be kind, but set boundaries now. A stuffed toy that the litter mates and mom have used is a great pacifier for the first few nights. Don't give in to the whining and crying, but shower them with attention and love. Weims thrive on companionship. You are their new mom and litter mate!*
>
> TONI FOW
> *Wing It Weimaraners*
>
> *A good tip is to have something that simulates the sound of a heartbeat. Weimaraners, unlike other breeds, tend to pile up and sleep on each other. So having that sound imitating a heartbeat helps with the transition.*
>
> JOE WIDOMSKI
> *Shades of Grey Weimaraners*

No two dogs are the same, so you may need to take several different approaches. What is consistent among the recommendations from breeders is not to give in to those yelps and whines. Once you do, it's over. Your dog is going to know that it will work, and his whining and barking will be endless. Yes, it is going to be incredibly challenging those first few nights, but after a week or two, your dog will learn that nighttime is for sleeping and that you will be there for him—he isn't alone.

Create a sleeping area for your puppy near where you sleep. The area should have the puppy's bed tucked safely into his crate. This will offer him a safe place to hide and a place where he will feel more comfortable in this strange new home. The entire area should be blocked off to be sure no one can get in (and the puppy can't get out) during the night. This sleeping area should also be close to where people sleep so that the puppy doesn't feel abandoned. If you were able to get a blanket or pillow that smells like the dog's mother, make sure that this is in your puppy's space. Consider adding a little white noise (like an old-fashioned alarm clock) to cover unfamiliar sounds that could scare your new pet.

Your puppy will make noises over the course of the night. Don't move the puppy away, even if the whimpering keeps you awake. Being moved away from people will only scare him more, reinforcing the feeling of anxiety. When your puppy whines during the night, he is not whimpering because he's been in the crate too long. He's scared or wants someone to be with him—he's probably never been alone at night before coming to live with you. Spare yourself trouble later on by teaching the puppy that whimpering will not get him out of the crate. Over time, being close to you at night will be enough to reassure your puppy that everything will be fine.

In the beginning, puppies will need to go to the bathroom every two to three hours. This means you will also need to get up during the night! Make sure your puppy understands he must always go to the bathroom outside or on the pee pad before bedtime. If you ignore this rule, you will have a tough time training your dog to only relieve himself when he is outside and not in the house.

If you choose to let your dog on the bed, wait until he is house-trained. Otherwise, you might have to replace your mattress within a short time. It is best to simply keep your Weimaraner off the furniture so that he doesn't get hurt and your furniture doesn't get ruined!

CHAPTER 8

Introducing Your Weimaraner to Your Other Dogs

Weimaraners tend to be more than happy to meet new dogs. If you rescue an older dog, an introduction may be a bit more challenging, depending on the dog's previous exposure to other canines. That enthusiasm, coupled with a lack of training, can be difficult for other dogs to handle. Whatever the age of your new Weimaraner, you will want to take the same steps to introduce him to your current dogs. Nearly all dogs are hesitant initially when they meet another canine in a completely new environment. If you have other dogs, it is a chance to begin socializing with your new Weimaraner (Chapter 12).

Chapter 8: Introducing Your Weimaraner to Your Other Dogs

If you already have a socialized adult dog, your current dog can also help teach your new Weimaraner the rules, and he could even become a mentor to your puppy. If you adopt a puppy, he may imitate your current dog's obedience when you give directions, something that could be really helpful with a potentially stubborn breed. However, this works both ways. If your current dog displays negative behavior, you should try to correct these habits before your puppy arrives. You don't want your Weimaraner pup learning bad habits.

As tempting as it may be, it is best not to bring two puppies into the home at the same time, especially from the same litter. They are much more likely to have a stronger bond with each other than with you or your family. Taking on one puppy at a time and having an adult to help you with that puppy is much more likely to have the best results. With a breed like the Weimaraner, two puppies at a time are going to be darn near impossible to handle unless you can be with them full-time for a couple of months. Having one high-energy, intelligent dog is going to be enough of a challenge. Having two means they can play off each other and make things a lot harder, as well as encourage each other to do things you definitely do not want them to do.

Do NOT have your dogs meet at a dog park. A dog park will just be a distraction for the initial meeting because of the number of other dogs coming and going. Find a quieter place to meet, and try to ensure that your dogs can focus on meeting each other instead of trying to go play in the dog area.

Introducing Your New Puppy to Your Other Pets

It doesn't matter what breed your new dog is—introducing him to your current dogs is always something that should be planned and monitored. Even if you feel you know your current dogs, bringing a new dog into the mix can be a challenge. This section details the best way to introduce a puppy to your dogs in an environment that should remove a lot of the potential issues that may make dogs fight.

> **HELPFUL TIP**
> **Social Precautions**
>
> Weimaraners typically get along well with other dogs if they are socialized well at a young age. Still, these hunting dogs are generally unsuitable for homes with other small animals or cats. Because of their high prey drive, Weimaraners frequently display animosity toward rodents, cats, birds, and reptiles. Exceptions to this exist, especially when Weimaraners are exposed to small animals as puppies. Still, extreme caution should be exercised when introducing a Weimaraner to other small pets in the home.

Introduce all new dogs to your current dog or dogs, regardless of age, in a neutral place away from your home. Even if you have never had problems with your current dog, you are about to change his world. When introducing your dog to the new puppy, select a park or other public area so your current dog will not feel territorial. Neutral ground provides a safer place for all canine parties to start getting to know each other.

When introducing the two dogs, make sure you have at least one other adult with you so that there's one person for each canine. All dogs should be leashed so that you can quickly and easily move them apart if the introduction does not go well. If you have more than two dogs, then you should have one adult per dog. You should not let more than one dog at a time meet your puppy because he may feel overwhelmed. When one of your dogs is through sniffing and meeting the puppy, you can let the next dog have a chance to meet the puppy. Let the dogs take turns meeting the puppy. This will make it easier to keep all of the dogs under control. Even the best dogs can get excited about meeting a puppy. One of the people who needs to be at this meeting is the person who is in charge of the pets in your home. This helps establish the pack hierarchy.

Don't hold your puppy in your arms when the dogs meet. While you may want to protect the puppy, holding him has the opposite effect. Instead, your puppy will feel trapped, but if he is on the ground, he can run if he feels scared. Stand near the puppy with your feet a little bit apart so the dog can hide behind your legs if he decides he needs to escape.

All dogs should have a few minutes to sniff each other, making sure there is always some slack on each leash. Feeling like they can move freely helps dogs to relax, and they won't feel like you are trying to restrain them or force them into something. Your dog may want to play, or he might simply ignore the puppy. You need to let your dog dictate what happens next. If the dogs want to play, be careful your current dog doesn't accidentally hurt the puppy, and if your dog ends up ignoring the puppy after an initial sniff, that is fine too. If your dog is clearly unhappy, keep all of the dogs apart until everyone is comfortable with the meeting. Don't force the situation.

This introduction could take a while, depending on each individual dog's personality. The friendlier and more accepting your current dog is, the easier it will be to incorporate your new puppy into the home. For some dogs, a week is enough time to start feeling comfortable together. For other dogs, it could take a couple of months before they are fully accepting of a new puppy. Since this is a completely new dynamic for your dog, he may be angry with you for bringing this new bundle of energy into his life.

The older your current dog is, the more likely it is that a puppy will be an unwelcome addition. Older dogs can get cranky around a puppy that doesn't know when enough is enough! The goal is to make your puppy feel welcome and safe and to let your older dog know that your love for him is as strong as ever.

Once your new family member and the rest of the canine pack become acquainted and comfortable, you can head home. When you arrive, take the dogs into the yard and remove the leashes. Again, you will need one adult per dog, including the puppy. If the dogs are all right or are indifferent to the puppy, you can let your current dog inside. Then re-leash the puppy, keeping him on the leash as you go inside. This is also a good time to take the puppy to the bathroom before going in so that he knows where to go.

Put the puppy in the puppy area when the introductions are completed. Remember to make sure your current dog cannot get into this area, and your puppy cannot get out.

Continuing to expose your puppy or adult dog to your other dogs is going to be important over the next few months. Puppies, in particular, need that socialization to learn not to be overprotective or wary of other pets in your home. Soon that puppy is going to be 80 pounds, bounding around the home, largely unaware of the chaos he causes. Older dogs

will almost certainly be annoyed by this. Younger, more energetic dogs may think the puppy is fun, which is great outside, but inside, it is likely to result in damage to your home. All encounters will need to be monitored for a few months until all canines have a more predictable relationship.

Introducing an Adult Dog to Other Pets

Always approach the introduction (and the first few weeks together) with caution. The new adult Weimaraner will need his own things from the very beginning—Weimaraners can be territorial if not properly trained. When you aren't around, your dog should be kept in a separate area so there won't be any fighting among the dogs. One thing to note is that some experts recommend you do not have two adult Weimaraners of the same sex together or even two adult dogs of the same gender, as they may not get along.

Plan for this introduction to take at least an hour. Since the dogs are both adults, they will need to move and become acquainted at their own pace. Since adult Weimaraners are less likely to be friendly initially (if not socialized or accustomed to other dogs), it could take longer. There should be some level of comfort before you leave the park to head home.

When introducing your current dog(s) to your new dog, follow the same steps as you would with a puppy:

Chapter 8: Introducing Your Weimaraner to Your Other Dogs

- Begin in neutral territory.
- Ask one adult to be present for each adult canine during the introduction.
- Introduce one dog at a time. Don't let several dogs meet your new Weimaraner all at once.

Bring treats to the meeting of two adult dogs—unlike with puppies. The animals will respond to the treats, and if the atmosphere becomes tense, the treats will create a distraction.

During the introduction, watch the Weimaraner and your dog(s) to see if any of them raise their hackles. This is one of the first obvious signs that a dog is uncomfortable. If the Weimaraner's hackles are up, back off the introductions for a little bit. Do this by calling your current dog back first. This is also when you should start waving treats around! Avoid pulling on the leashes to separate the dogs. You don't want to add physical tension to the situation because that could trigger a fight. Treats will work for all dogs, and calling their names should help get things under control.

If any of the dogs are showing their teeth or growling, call your dog back and give the animals a chance to settle down. Use treats and a calming voice to get them to relax. You want all the dogs to feel comfortable during the first meeting, so don't force the friendship. If they seem uncomfortable or wary at first, let them move at their own pace.

Older Dogs and Your Weimaraner

If your current dog is older, keep in mind puppies are energetic, and they want to engage older dogs in play. This can be very trying for your older canine, so make sure your older dog doesn't get too tired of the puppy's antics. A tired older dog could snap and nip at your puppy in hopes of getting a little rest. You don't want your puppy to begin snapping at other dogs too. Watch for signs your older dog is ready for some alone time, some time with you, or simply a break from the puppy. Given how energetic and noisy Weimaraners can be, you want to ensure that your older dog has a place to hide away so that he can relax.

You should always make sure your older dog has safe places to be alone. This is essential for those times he just doesn't feel up to being around a spry, young puppy! By keeping your puppy and your older dog separated, you can prevent the need for constant scolding. Plus, the puppy will not become wary of older dogs.

Even if you rescue an adult Weimaraner, he might still be too energetic for your older dog to handle. Weimaraners tend to mellow when they mature, but there are some that tend to love being active until they get close to their senior years. Given the size of an adult, that energy will probably come off as incredibly annoying to your older dogs. Be mindful and make sure your dog's golden years are not marred by a new canine that wants to play in a way your older dog can't anymore. Weimaraners are more likely to understand limits faster than a lot of other breeds, but you want to minimize how annoyed your older dog is while your puppy is learning the boundaries.

Dog Aggression and Territorial Behavior

Weimaraners may exhibit a level of dominance or aggression toward dogs they don't know, but usually, this is only a concern when a Weimaraner isn't properly socialized. This is one of the primary reasons why you should never let your Weimaraner off-leash—the other reason being the dog may be a bit too excited and probably won't return because there is too much to explore if he is off-leash. (Details on how to train your Weimaraner are discussed in Chapter 11.)

Dominance aggression is when your dog wants to show control over another animal or person. This kind of aggression can be seen in the following behaviors and in reaction to anyone going near the Weimaraner's belongings (like toys or a food bowl):

- Growling
- Nipping
- Snapping

This is the behavior that pack leaders use to warn others not to touch their stuff. If you see this reaction in your Weimaraner while he's around you, a family member, or another pet, you must intervene immediately. Correct him by saying, "No," then lavish him with praise when the behavior stops. You must consistently intervene whenever your Weimaraner behaves in this manner.

Do not leave your Weimaraner alone with other people, dogs, or animals as long as any dominance aggression is exhibited. If you are not there to intervene, your dog will push boundaries and will likely try to show his dominance over those around him. Never train your Weimaraner to react aggressively!

Once you are sure this behavior has been eliminated, you can leave your current dog and Weimaraner alone for short periods of time. You should remain in another room or somewhere in close proximity but out of sight. Over time, you can leave your pets alone when you get the mail; then, try leaving them when you run errands or longer tasks. Eventually, you will be able to safely leave your Weimaraner alone with other dogs.

Feeding Time Practices

Your Weimaraner puppy will be fed in his puppy space, so mealtime will not be a problem in the beginning. If you can feed him in his crate, that could be very helpful. However, by the end of the first year, you should be able to have all of your dogs eating in the same area, and that requires some planning and preparation. With a Weimaraner, it will also mean having a towel handy to clean up after all of the slobbering over food ends.

The following are suggestions for feeding your puppy when the other dogs are present; this will reduce the chances of territorial behavior:

- Feed your Weimaraner at the same time as the other dogs but in a different room. Keeping them separated will let your Weimaraner eat without distractions or feeling that your other dogs will eat what is in his bowl. Make sure to feed your Weimaraner in the same room each time while the other dogs eat in their established areas.
- Keep your Weimaraner and other dogs in their areas until they finish eating their food. Some dogs have a tendency to leave food in the bowl. Don't let them. They need to finish everything because all food bowls will be removed as soon as the dogs finish eating. If food is left, get the bowl off the ground.
- Make sure you have someone near your Weimaraner so that the dog learns not to growl at people near the bowl. This will help reduce stress when other dogs are around the food. If your dog demonstrates any aggression, immediately correct him by saying, "No," and then give praise when the behavior stops. Do not play with the food bowl, and make sure none of the kids play with it. Your dog needs to know that no one is going to try to steal his food.
- Over the course of a couple of weeks, move your dogs closer together while they are eating. For example, you can feed your current dog on one side of the door near the doorway and the Weimaraner on the opposite side.

Chapter 8: Introducing Your Weimaraner to Your Other Dogs

- After a month or two, you can feed the dogs in the same room but with some distance between them. If your Weimaraner starts to exhibit protective behavior with the other dogs, correct the Weimaraner and then praise him when he stops the behavior.

Eventually, you can start feeding the dogs close to one another. This can take weeks to months to accomplish, depending on the age of the Weimaraner and his personality. A puppy will need less time because he will be socialized with the dogs from an early age, making him less wary that the other dogs will try to take his food. That does not mean he won't display territorial behavior. Yet, it likely won't take long for him to start to feel comfortable eating near the rest of the pack.

For adult dogs, this process could take longer—don't rush it! Let your dog learn to feel comfortable eating before you make changes, even small ones. Dogs of any breed can be protective of their food, depending on their past history. Before your dog will eat peacefully, he must be assured that his protective behavior is not necessary around other dogs. That means letting his confidence and comfort level build at his own pace.

Cleaning up behind your Weimaraner's meal can be helpful. Any slobber and water on the floor could be a slippery hazard, and slobber on the walls will build up and create discoloration over time. This is a consideration for many dogs because some breeds slobber a lot more than others, but with a dog as big as a Weimaraner, the mess is going to be a lot more obvious after every meal. The cleanup won't take long—just a quick wipe down, then you can get back to having fun with your dog.

Photo Courtesy of Gina Roessler

CHAPTER 9

The First Few Weeks

With a Weimaraner in the home, time is going to fly because their enthusiasm is contagious. Your new dog will keep you on your toes and entertained, so try to stop and enjoy it when you can. Your dog's personality will start to show, and you'll learn what kinds of rewards and incentives work well in getting your Weimaraner to listen. This process is not going to be easy; it is absolutely a lot of work, especially during the first week, as you try to train your dog while making sure he feels comfortable in his new surroundings. Leaving his previous home, even for a rescue, is going to make the dog apprehensive about being somewhere new. There are a lot of things to do (and some

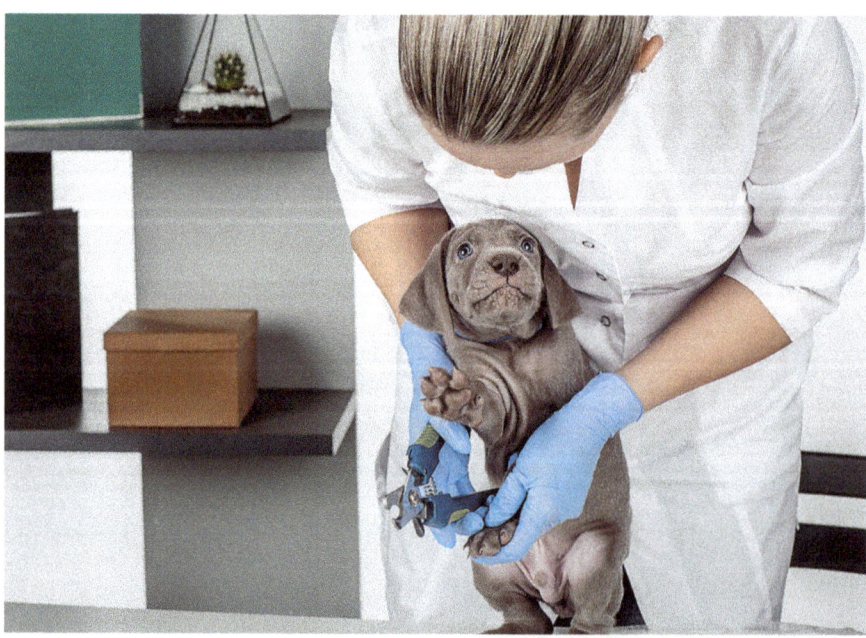

things to avoid) to help your dog ease into the new environment and really bring out his excited, active, and loving personality. During that first week, it is about helping your dog feel comfortable enough not to be wary of the new setting.

As mentioned in the previous chapter, there shouldn't be much training outside of crate training and house-training during those first few weeks. Puppies don't listen during the early days when the instructions aren't for something they do naturally. They will definitely need to use the bathroom and eat, so crate training and house-training are things they will understand. Also, they haven't learned to listen to you yet. You can avoid creating a negative training environment by giving yourself and your dog time to get acquainted before you dive into other types of training. Don't worry; your dog isn't really going to lose time because Weimaraners are clever. With your bond established, it will be easier to get your dog to take you more seriously instead of being wary.

With their intelligence, Weimaraners will likely quickly understand their new surroundings as they learn that this is their new home. When your dog is not sleeping, you may find yourself feeling that you can't get a moment's rest—but in a fun and entertaining way. The bond you and your Weimaraner form in those early days will be important in establishing the relationship you have over the years.

By the end of the first month, your pup should be sleeping through the night, which will be an absolute blessing considering how difficult those first few days tend to be. House-training can be very easy when it is done right, but without the right approach, it can be a real chore. Having a great breeder who starts the process will further speed up how quickly your little one learns. You will want to monitor your Weimaraner, though, and never let a puppy or dog out of the dedicated area alone during the first week and probably a good bit longer.

> ## CELEBRITY WEIMARANER
> ### Grace Kelly's Dogs
>
> When American actress Grace Kelly married Prince Rainier III of Monaco in 1956, she received a Weimaraner as a wedding gift from her brother. The pair were photographed together several times, but unfortunately, this dog's name has been lost to history.

The first month is when you really need to start paying attention to your puppy's emerging personality. As with all intelligent breeds, the key is to remain consistent when it comes to training. That means everyone should be consistent, including the kids. Always use what you learn about your puppy's personality to encourage good behavior!

Setting the Rules and Sticking to Them

> The smart ones are always watching and always looking for a way to cheat. Consistency and repetition are key in training. Even if a dog is well trained and absolutely knows what it should or shouldn't be doing, the minute you aren't paying attention, the Weim will take advantage of it and will get into mischief.
>
> JESSICA HANSON
> Hanson Weimaraners

If Weimaraners see that people are willing to compromise, they are going to exploit that as much as possible. By making exceptions, the lesson they are learning is how to get you to do what they want. A good rule for any breed, but especially for larger and more intelligent dogs, is to always set the rules and a schedule and don't allow any deviation. This goes for both your dog and your kids, regardless of the age of the dog or child. You don't want your older children or teens undoing your hard work by letting the new Weimaraner out of the puppy's dedicated area to roam around unattended. Make sure everyone knows that the rules apply to everyone.

Rules are not the same as more traditional training. The rules are the same as the kinds of rules you give your children; other types of training are more like what kids learn in school. It's never too early to start teaching your dog the rules.

Your puppy needs to understand the rules and know you and your family mean them, even if the dog really doesn't like what you are saying.

Chapter 9: The First Few Weeks

Once your canine learns to follow your commands, there will still be times when he will refuse to obey. That is nearly a certainty. However, he will be much more likely to listen once he knows you are in control.

Do not allow yourself or anyone in your family to think that making an exception is all right, no matter how cute those eyes are. Once a Weimaraner realizes that certain rules are negotiable, it will be incredibly difficult to teach him otherwise. The best reward is positive reinforcement, not breaking the rules.

Photo Courtesy of Michael Bill

Establish a No Jumping and No Mouthing Policy

No matter how cute your puppy might be, you definitely want to start training your dog not to jump up on people because once he reaches his full height and weight, he will be able to knock people off their feet. If not properly trained, a Weimaraner may jump up on you in greeting, and this can be very bad if the dog tries to jump up on little children or frail adults. Such a sturdy build means the dog can easily knock over a toddler unintentionally. You have the responsibility of ensuring that your dog and children learn how to play properly. For your Weimaraner, this means no jumping up on people.

Nor do you want a puppy to feel it is all right to mouth you because when your dog is fully grown, his mouth is going to be enormous. Any games that involve biting or nipping should always be avoided. You do not want your Weimaraner to ever think that nipping is all right. This will be very difficult if you don't enforce the rule right from the beginning.

Nipping

Although they aren't generally aggressive, Weimaraners (or any dog) are likely to nip under two conditions.
- One of the triggers for nipping is overstimulation. This can be one sign your puppy is too tired to keep playing or training, and you should put him to bed.
- Another trigger could be that your canine has too much energy. If this is the case, take your puppy outside to burn off some of his excess energy. At the same time, be careful not to over-exercise the puppy.

You need to be vigilant and immediately let your puppy know nipping is not acceptable. Some people recommend using a water spritzer bottle and spraying the puppy while saying "No," after nipping. This is one of the few times when punishment may be effective, and it is probably essential. Remember—make sure your dog does not associate the spraying with anything other than his nipping. He needs to understand that he is getting sprayed because he is nipping someone and that this is not acceptable behavior.

Always firmly tell your puppy, "No," whenever he is nipping, even if it is during playtime. You should also pull away and loudly say, "Ouch!" to let your puppy know his teeth are hurting you. This will help to establish the idea that nipping is bad and is never rewarded.

Chewing

All puppies chew to relieve the pain of teething. Whether your dog is chewing on your furniture or clothing, be sure to discourage this behavior as quickly as possible:
- Make sure you have toys for your Weimaraner (whether an adult or a puppy) so that you can teach him what objects are acceptable for chewing. Having a lot of available toys and rotating those toys out will give your puppy or dog several options.

Chapter 9: The First Few Weeks

Photo Courtesy of Gloria Bryant

- If your puppy is teething, either refrigerate a couple of toys so that they are cold or give your puppy frozen carrots. The cold will help to numb the pain. Teething usually starts between three and four months old, and it usually ends by eight months. You want to get toys that will be safe for your dog's teeth.
- Toys that are made of hard rubber or hard nylon are best, particularly Kongs with kibble in them. You can even fill them with water and freeze them, which will give your puppy something cool to soothe the pain of teething.

For the most part, keeping an eye on your dog when he is not in his designated space will help you quickly see when he is chewing on things he shouldn't. When this happens, firmly say, "No." If your dog continues to chew, put him back in his space. While he is in the space, make sure he has plenty of toys to chew on.

If you decide to use chew deterrents, such as bitter training sprays, be aware some dogs will not care if an item tastes bad—they will chew on it anyway. If you apply these deterrents, do not leave your dog alone and expect him to stop chewing. You should watch your dog's reaction before trusting that the bad habit is broken. Since some Weimaraners have separation anxiety, you should eliminate the chewing problem as quickly as possible; this will allow your pup to roam freely around your home.

Jumping

As noted earlier, you should not allow your Weimaraner to jump up on other people or animals. A cute little puppy will be able to knock down full-grown adults within a year, and this can be detrimental to everyone involved. Use the following steps when you have a visitor. If you can, get someone who is willing to help you because that will make training that much easier; two people will be able to better handle a large dog.

1. Put a leash on the dog when the person knocks on the door or rings the bell. The arrival of someone will invariably excite most dogs, especially puppies.
2. Let the person in, but do not approach the visitor until your pup calms down.
3. Be effusive in your praise when the puppy keeps all four paws on the ground.
4. If the puppy jumps up on the visitor, the visitor should turn his body and ignore the dog. Don't verbally correct the dog. Being completely ignored will be far more of a deterrent than any words you can say.
5. Give your dog something to hold in his mouth if he does not settle down. Sometimes dogs just need a task to reduce their

excitement. A stuffed animal or a ball is an ideal distraction, even if your dog drops it.
6. At this point, the visitor can get down to the dog's level and pet your dog. Having someone on his level will make your Weimaraner feel he is being included. It also lets him sniff the visitor's face, which is part of a proper greeting to a dog. If your visitor is willing to help, this acknowledgment can prevent your pup from further jumping since he already feels safe with the person who is at his level.

Reward-Based Training Versus Discipline-Based Training

> *Remember how intelligent they are? Use it to your advantage! Gentle, loving, but firm consistency with all training is the key. Lots of exuberance with Good boy/girl if good, and firm NO if doing something not desired, then redirect the dog to something else. Remember the toddler. Above all, be patient. The puppy is learning how to adjust to a brand-new home and routine without its litter-mates, mother, and breeder.*
>
> KYRA SCHLIEMAN
> *SilverLining Weimaraners*

With an intelligent breed like the Weimaraner, it is much more efficient to train your puppy using rewards than with punishments. This will be a particular challenge as puppies can be exuberant and easily distracted. It is important to remember that your puppy is young, so you need to keep your temper and learn when a break from training is needed. Since Weimaraners are interested in pleasing their people, positive attention can be incredibly effective in getting your dog to listen to you.

The following are several critical training aspects you will need to address during the first month:
- House-training (Chapter 10)
- Crate training (Chapter 6)
- Barking (Chapter 11)

Find out how much house-training was completed by the breeder. The best breeders may teach puppies one or two commands before the puppy goes home with you. If this is the case, keep using those same commands with your puppy so that the early training is not lost. This information can help you establish the right tone of voice to use with your puppy since he will already know what the words mean and how to react to them.

How Long Is Too Long to Be Left Home Alone?

> *Weims can be prone to separation anxiety. Start when the dog is young, teaching it that being alone is a normal part of everyday life. Do this by crate training, leaving the dog alone in the house in a crate for gradually longer periods of time.*
>
> **ANNE TYSON**
> *Regen Weimaraners*

Weimaraners suffer from separation anxiety, and that means leaving them home alone for long periods of time is not advised. Some of them can learn to be all right while you are away for a full workday. Others never seem to get to the point where hours of separation are easy to take.

In the beginning, your dog should spend only a brief period of time in the crate while you are gone. Weimaraners have been companions

Chapter 9: The First Few Weeks

Photo Courtesy of Trichelle Mattas

since they were first bred, so they do not like to be left home alone. This is why it is best to make sure they have a companion. As your dog becomes house-trained and trustworthy, you should allow him to leave the crate while you are gone so that he doesn't feel he is being punished. Your new companion will not do well trapped in a crate for hours at a time. That said, in an emergency, a dog can be all right in a crate for up to eight hours without a person as long as you have made sure to allow the dog to burn off energy first.

You also need to find some good mental games that will keep your pup occupied while you are gone. Brain games can keep your dog happily occupied while you are away, and having another dog can provide stimulation (though you may want to make sure to tire them both out before leaving, and the companion dog must also be well-socialized and not of the same gender).

Don't Overdo It – Physically or Mentally

As an adult, your Weimaraner will probably be highly active. As a puppy, your Weimaraner will go from sleeping to being rambunctious to sleeping again, all within a brief period of time. A tired puppy is a lot like a tired toddler; you have to keep the little guy from becoming exhausted or from overworking those short little legs (while they are still short). You need to be careful about harming your puppy's growing bones. Your pup is probably going to think that sleep is unnecessary, no matter how tired he is. It is up to you to read the signs that tell you when to stop all activities and take a break or put your pup to bed.

You should train your dog in increments of time—only for the amount of time that he can handle. Don't push your puppy's training past his concentration level, and don't discourage your adult dog by using commands that are too advanced. If you continue training your puppy past his energy levels, the lessons learned are not going to be the ones you want to teach your dog. At this age, training sessions don't need to be long; they just need to be consistent.

Walks will be much shorter during the first month. When you go outside, stay within a few blocks of home. Don't worry—by the month's end,

Chapter 9: The First Few Weeks

your puppy will have more stamina, and you will be able to enjoy longer walks with your new friend. You can also do a bit of walking on the leash in the yard if your puppy has lots of extra energy. Puppies have a tendency to attack their leash while walking because it is a distraction from running freely. Taking walks will also help your Weimaraner learn how to behave on the leash.

Just because your puppy can't endure long walks initially doesn't mean he won't have plenty of energy. Daily exercise will be essential, with the caveats that you need to make sure your puppy isn't doing too much too soon and that he doesn't get too hot. Staying active will not only keep him healthy, but it will also keep him mentally stimulated. You will quickly realize how sedentary your "non-puppy life" has been because you will be on the move the entire time your puppy is awake!

Photo Courtesy of Charles Rudziewicz

PART 3
Training and Activities

CHAPTER 10

House-training

Now it's time to consider what is probably the least enjoyable aspect of having a puppy – house training. Even if it is nobody's favorite task, everyone can appreciate the successful end results of house training a puppy because it means far less mess to clean up. After those first few months, the effort will be more than worth it when you no longer have to worry about hidden messes around your home.

This task doesn't have to be particularly difficult, especially since Weimaraners tend to have fairly predictable bathroom schedules; you just need to make sure to get them outside as soon as they wake up. Since he's a food-driven dog, giving your Weimaraner treats after using

the bathroom outside is going to help him make the connection pretty easily in the early days. Within half a year, a well-trained Weimaraner is very unlikely to have accidents.

You need to treat house-training with the same kind of patience and consistency that you apply to other types of training. This does tend to be more difficult because we want to punish "bad behavior," but in the early days, using the inside of the house to do their business isn't "bad" – it's natural. Consider that humans aren't even able to be potty trained until they can walk, which is usually about two years after they are born—six months doesn't seem quite so long when you put it in perspective. Keep in mind that your Weimaraner isn't misbehaving or intentionally disobeying you; he is learning where to go to the restroom, which is a lot harder than learning how to sit. To speed up the process, be patient, and praise your dog when he goes in the right place. Your dog wants to please you, so treats and positive reinforcement will go a long way to getting your Weimaraner to use the outside for all of that potty business.

The recommended age to start house-training a Weimaraner is between eight and nine weeks, although this is a breed that can get started around 5 weeks – that's how intelligent they are. Since you probably aren't going to see that much progress very early though, you can start showing him other dogs going outside to relieve themselves. Weimaraners likely won't have enough bladder and bowel control to be consistent until they are at least 8 weeks old.

While you are trying to train the dog on where to use the bathroom, you will almost certainly see your dog trying to decide if he should listen to you. All it takes is one time when you allow yourself to be distracted, and you can turn house-training into an incredibly difficult chore. But if you can keep your focus while remaining consistent and firm, your Weimaraner should be trained by the time he's six months old.

> *Weimaraners thrive on praise! Also having a bell on a door within nose reach that they can signal to go outside helps.*
>
> **JOE WIDOMSKI**
> *Shade of Grey Weimaraners*

Staying focused when you have your dog outside for a restroom break isn't necessarily enough; if you fail to keep a constant eye on your puppy when he is exploring inside your home, be prepared for a lot of messes. Puppies will sneak off to use the bathroom inside if you let your attention stray.

This is when learning to be firm and consistent is really going to count, and sticking to the rules will be absolutely essential. You will also need

to remain calm and patient; getting upset will only reinforce undesirable behavior. The best tool in house-training a potentially stubborn breed is to set a schedule and stick to it—no deviations! Once your dog realizes you are staying focused and that you will get him outside for a break, he will accept that rule and do what he's supposed to do.

Leashing your Weimaraner to go outside can help show your puppy where and when to go to the bathroom—even in your yard. However, there will still be challenges.

The following is a list of rules to apply when house-training your puppy:
- Never let the puppy roam the house alone—he should always be in his dedicated puppy space when you are not watching him. No Weimaraner wants to spend a lot of time in a soiled crate, so being in his crate is a deterrent from doing his business there when you are not around. He may not feel the same way about other areas of your home if he is free to wander.
- Give your puppy constant, easy access to his designated bathroom spaces. You will need to make frequent trips outside with your puppy as he learns where to do his business.

- When you go outside, put a leash on your puppy to make a point of where in the yard you want him to use the bathroom.
- If your puppy doesn't potty within a few minutes, take him inside and put him in the crate for a few minutes. Then take him back outside to make sure he does go to the bathroom. This isn't punishment for the puppy but a break in case he was getting too distracted to focus on going to the bathroom. Once all of those stimuli are removed, and he's in his crate, he may realize that he does have some business to take care of.

Always begin with a training plan; then, be even stricter with yourself than you are with your puppy when keeping to the schedule. You are the key to your puppy's learning!

> *If 2-3 weeks go by and you're not seeing progress, or if the puppy seems to be going more frequently or having accidents in the house may need to have them checked for a urinary tract infection, especially if female.*
>
> **KYRA SCHIEMANN**
> *Silver Lining Weimaraner*

Inside or Outside – House-training Options and Considerations

If your breeder has already started the house-training process, make sure to coordinate your training so that you pick up where the breeder left off. Having someone who really knows how to house-train a dog can give you a huge leg up on the whole endeavor—take it if you can get it!

The following is a list of house-training options for your puppy:
- Pee pads – You should have several around the home for training, including in the puppy's area but as far from his bed as possible.

- Regular outings – Organize these outings based on your puppy's sleeping and eating schedule.
- Rewards – You can use treats in the beginning but quickly shift to praise.

Setting a Schedule

You need to keep an eye on your puppy and always follow his meals, before and after sleep, and before and after being in his crate, with house-training sessions. Watch for cues like sniffing and circling, which are two common signs a puppy exhibits when searching for a place to go potty. Start tailoring your schedule around your puppy's unique needs. Puppies have small bladders and little control in the early days—so at this time, it isn't stubbornness but ability that is making it difficult for your puppy to follow your directions.

> *Pups need to do their business often - after waking, after eating, after playing. Give them frequent access to the area you would like them to use to potty and do your very best to prevent accidents. If you see them sniffing, circling, leaving the room to explore, wandering near the door, looking frantic, or running aimlessly take them outside. Praise them for doing their business outdoors.*
>
> ANNE TYSON
> *Regen Weimaraners*

If you train your pup to do his business inside, you need a designated space in the puppy's area for a clean pee pad. Pee pads are better than newspapers and can absorb more. Make sure you change the pads regularly so that your puppy does not get accustomed to having waste nearby. Even if you use pee pads, you should plan to transition your dog to doing his business outdoors as quickly as possible.

Chapter 10: House-training

Choosing a Location

> *Crate, schedule, and routines. Keep a close eye on the dog at all times. If it's cold in winter where you are, litter box train using a kiddie pool in the garage, on the patio, or another area the dog can access that is not in the house but is more comfortable than out in the snow.*
>
> JESSICA HANSON
> *Hanson Weimaraners*

A designated bathroom space will make the house-training experience easier because your Weimaraner will associate one area of the yard with that specific purpose. Having him use one spot every time will also make clean-up simpler, and you will be able to use the entire yard instead of having to worry about stepping in dog waste.

The perfect time to train your puppy to go to the bathroom is when you go out for walks. Between walks and using the yard, your puppy will come to see the leash as a sign that it is time to relieve his bladder, which could become a Pavlovian response.

Do not send your puppy outside alone and assume he has done what you want him to do. He needs to understand the purpose of going outside is to go to the bathroom. Until there are no more accidents in the house, you need to be sure your puppy is not losing focus. With a breed like the Weimaraner, it is best to always verify that your little fellow follows through. If it is too hot or cold outside and you don't make sure he takes care of business, you run the risk that he will take advantage of that lack of supervision to pretend he

Photo Courtesy of Walt Freshour

has done his business just so he can get back inside faster. Then accidents are nearly guaranteed, even if you thought that your dog was fully house-trained.

Key Word Training

All training should include key words, even house-training. You and all family members should consistently use key words when house-training your dog. If you have paired an adult with a child, the adult should be the one using the key word during training.

To avoid confusing your puppy, be careful not to select words that you often use inside the home. Use a phrase like "Get busy" to let your puppy know it's time to do his business. Do not use words like "bathroom" or "potty" because these words are sometimes used in casual conversation, which could trigger a desire in your dog to go to the bathroom. "Get busy" is not a phrase most people use in their daily routine, so it is not something you are likely to say unless you want your puppy to go to the bathroom outside.

Once your puppy learns to use the bathroom based on the command, make sure he finishes before offering praise or rewards.

Reward Good Behavior with Positive Reinforcement

> *Make it fun for your puppy with everything you do, lavishly praise the good behavior, and have special treats to offer periodically to reinforce desired behavior.*
>
> **KYRA SCHLIEMAN**
> *SilverLining*

Weimaraners are incredibly receptive to positive reinforcement, making it highly effective for all kinds of training (not just house-training). In the beginning, take a few pieces of kibble with you when you are teaching your puppy where to go, both inside and outside the home. Learning you are the one in charge will help teach your Weimaraner to look to you for cues and instructions.

Part of being consistent with training means lavishing the little guy with praise whenever your puppy does the right thing. Use a leash to gently lead your puppy to his bathroom area, with no stops in between. It will gradually become obvious to your Weimaraner that this is where he should go to use the bathroom. Once you get outside, encourage your pup to go only when you get to the place in the yard that is intended for his bathroom spot. As soon as he does his business, give him immediate and very enthusiastic praise. Pet your puppy as you talk, and let the little guy know just how good the action was. Once the praise is done, return inside immediately. This is not playtime. You want your puppy to associate certain outings with designated potty time.

While praise is incredibly effective with Weimaraners, you can also give your puppy a treat after a few successful trips outside. Definitely do not make treats a habit after each trip because you do not want your Weimaraner to expect one every time he does his business. The lesson is to go outside, not to receive a treat every time.

The best way to house-train in the first couple of months is to go out every hour or two, even during the night. Set an alarm to wake yourself during the night so that you remember to take the puppy outside. Use the leash to keep the focus on using the bathroom, give the same enthusiastic praise, then immediately return inside and go back to bed. It is

> **FUN FACT**
> **The Gray Ghost**
>
> Weimaraners have earned the nickname "gray ghosts" due to their silver coloring and propensity for stealth. Weimaraners are excellent trackers and have been described as catlike in their pursuit. According to the AKC, Weimaraners have also been known to "hide their scent" by rolling in odorous substances or mud. Therefore, keeping plenty of dog shampoo (and patience) on hand for these messy endeavors is never a bad idea.

difficult, but your Weimaraner will get the hang of it a lot faster if there isn't a lengthy period between potty breaks. Over time, the pup will need to go outside less frequently.

Cleaning Up

> *The best-suited family for a Weim is ... one that is not too serious about their landscaping and doesn't get bent out of shape over slobbery wet floors and muddy paw prints.*
>
> **JESSICA HANSON**
> *Hanson Weimaraners*

Once a dog goes to the bathroom in your home, that odor will remain there for other dogs to smell, even if it's not detectable to your own nose after you've cleaned the area thoroughly. Your Weimaraner might take any lingering odor as a sign that the spot is an acceptable place to use the bathroom.

This means you have to be very diligent about handling accidents:
- Clean up any messes in the house as soon as you find them.
- In areas where your dog has an accident, thoroughly clean the spot so that there is no remaining scent.

Spend a bit of time researching what kind of cleaner you want to use, whether generic or holistic. For example, you will probably want to get a product with an enzyme cleaner. Enzymes help to remove stains by speeding up the chemical reaction of the cleaner with the stain. They also help to remove the smell faster, which reduces the odds your dog will continue to go to the bathroom in the same place. If your Weimaraner is properly trained, he will feel no need to mark his territory, but you should also discourage other dogs from claiming areas around your property.

If your Weimaraner has an accident, it is important to refrain from punishing the puppy. Punishment simply teaches your dog to hide

Chapter 10: House-training

Photo Courtesy of Dawn Scott

his mess or to be stealthier about when he does his business inside. Accidents are not a reason to punish. If they happen often, it is really more of a reflection of your training and your schedule than on the puppy. However, even the best trainers can tell you accidents are pretty much an inevitability. When it happens, tell your puppy, "No! Potty outside!" and clean up the mess immediately. Once you have finished cleaning the mess, take the puppy outside. It isn't likely that he will need to go potty again, but it is worth the attempt in case he still has a little left.

Pay attention to when these accidents happen, and determine if there is a commonality between them. Perhaps you need to add an extra trip outside during the day for your puppy, or you should make a change in his walking schedule. Or maybe there is something that is startling your dog and causing an accident.

Remember, this is a dog that is loyal and loves his people. As a people-pleaser, it is far easier to get a Weimaraner house-trained faster. If you get upset, that will upset your dog, resulting in more accidents. If you can stay calm and patient, house-training isn't going to be the nightmare that it can be with a lot of other breeds.

CHAPTER 11

Training Your Weimaraner

With the right approach, Weimaraners can be incredibly easy to train. Their desire to please their people coupled with a high food drive means that you have a wealth of tools at your disposal to get them to understand instructions. However, there is a good chance that your dog will believe he can outsmart you, making the training a little less straightforward.

> *The breed being very intelligent and stubborn can be both easy and difficult to train. My spouse, of German descent himself likes to say 'You have to say NO one more time than the dog wants to hear it.' But of course with consistency and love!*
>
> **KYRA SCHIEMANN**
> *Silver Lining Weimaraners*

Since they are intelligent, they don't tend to take that long to put two and two together. While you will need to be mindful of how many treats you give your Weimaraner when he's a puppy, he's going to be growing really fast, so getting the basics down quickly may mean giving him a lot of treats. Over time, you can move to praise (it will be pretty effective, too) as the primary reward, but to get your large dog to listen and understand the critical commands, giving treats will help speed up the learning process. When dealing with a dog as big as the Weimaraner, giving puppies more treats is all right. If you have an adult Weimaraner

Chapter 11: Training Your Weimaraner

that needs training, though, you are going to have to go light on the treats and primarily offer praise.

Positive attention and extra play are fantastic rewards for a loving dog like the Weimaraner, so training is still going to be relatively easy. As they are dogs that are very sensitive to any negativity, it is best not to agitate them because that will make them less likely to understand or do what you want.

It is absolutely essential to ensure that your Weimaraner learns the basic commands covered in these chapters for his protection and for that of your visitors. Given his size, a Weimaraner can get carried away and knock people over without any understanding of how dangerous his actions are.

Early Training is a Must

> Most Weim pups are food oriented. You can teach a puppy a lot when very young just with food rewards. These dogs love to be trained, so take advantage of that!
>
> ELENA LAMBERSON
> *Silversmith Weimaraners*

Photo Courtesy of Trichelle Mattas

All large dogs require early training because of the risks they pose if they don't learn how to behave. From knocking people over to literally running over children, large dogs are more likely to accidentally harm others. It can be difficult to stay composed when a dog keeps jumping up on people because most people don't know how to deal with this kind of behavior in an effective way. The natural reaction is to give a dog attention, even if it is to try to convince him to stay down. Training him early, before he spends much time outside with others, will help you to get some of the bad behaviors worked out. Given how different Weimaraners look from most other breeds, you'll find that a lot of people will approach your dog out of curiosity. Your Weimaraner will probably be just as curious about them, so you want to make sure that you are able to keep all four of his paws on the ground during social interactions.

Best Practices and Benefits to Keep in Mind before You Start

In the early days, be prepared to keep your frustration levels in check. Your dog has to be convinced that you are in charge and that you mean business—and he needs to know the reward for that is a lot of fun. If you take out your frustration on your Weimaraner, you are teaching him that training isn't fun. Whether you bring a puppy or an adult dog into your home, he has to learn the boundaries in a way that is safe and shows patience, just like teaching a child. If you take a few minutes to watch training videos of Weimaraners before you bring one home and as you prepare to start training, that will give you a good idea of what you could be in for when you start to train your newest family member.

Just remember—being firm, consistent, and patient will go a long way. Don't let that adorable face sway you from getting your pup to do what you instruct him to do. He will be just as happy a little way down the road if you stick to it now. And that happy face when playing with you is priceless.

Always make the early training sessions short, no matter how old your dog is. Those training sessions are as much about learning how your Weimaraner will respond to training as they are about actually training your dog. Puppies won't have the ability to keep focused like adults, so a short session is ideal for keeping them from learning to ignore you. Adult dogs are going to be suspicious of you (though you may also get an adult that is already familiar with training, which could make training a little easier). And odds are, you are going to be quite tired by the end of those sessions—you'll be just as relieved as your pup is to be done. As long as you are firm and consistent during those early sessions, keeping them short is in everyone's best interest.

> **FUN FACT**
> **The Nose Knows**
>
> Tracking is an ideal sport for Weimaraners due to their better-than-average sense of smell. In their early days as hunting dogs, Weimaraners relied on their keen noses to track large game in Germany. Today, Weimaraners can enjoy tracking for sport and compete in AKC tracking events, including the AKC National Tracking Invitational (NTI). For more information about AKC tracking training, visit www.ack.org/sports/tracking.

Training will be slow going in the beginning, as your dog will be quite excited about the interaction. Don't take this as an indication of your puppy's interest levels—it's more indicative of his inexperience. If you are patient with your pup from the start, you will find it will pay off later.

Training is as important as socialization, and it can make general excursions easier; more importantly, training could be a way of saving your dog's life. Understanding commands might prevent your dog from running into the street, responding to provocations from other dogs, or acting territorial.

Training can also really benefit your relationship with your pup because it is a wonderful way to bond. This dedicated time together helps you understand your puppy's developing personality as you learn what kind of reward will work best for other tasks. Be sure your Weimaraner is well-trained so you can enjoy a full range of activities together—from picnics to outings in the park!

Choosing the Right Reward

The right reward for a Weimaraner will ultimately be love and affection because these dogs adore their people. Treats are the easiest way of keying a puppy into the idea that performing tricks is good behavior, but ultimately you want your little one to follow commands without expecting food. Soon, you will need to switch to a reward that is a secondary reinforcer. Praise, additional playtime, and extra petting are all fantastic rewards for your Weimaraner. Your dog will probably follow you around until you decide to just sit back and relax. Plopping down to watch a movie and letting your puppy sit with you is a great reward after an intense training session.

> **"**
>
> *Weims are very food motivated and most of them also really want to please. It's important to be consistent, positive, and have frequent, short, training sessions when the pup is young. Teaching a reliable 'come' command to a young pup will pay dividends in the future.*
>
> ANNE TYSON
> *Regen Weimaraners*
>
> **"**

Make sure you switch from treats to a different kind of positive reward as early as possible. Since many Weimaraners love their toys, you don't have to rely solely on treats as a method of praise.

If you would like your Weimaraner to connect positive feedback with a sound, you can use a clicker. This training tool is relatively inexpensive and should be used at the same time as you praise your puppy or dog. Clickers are not necessary, but some trainers find them useful.

Name Recognition

Using a dog's name is going to be the first part of training your dog. Over time, many of us create different names for our dogs. Nicknames can be used later. However, before you can train a dog, you have to make sure he understands his real name. In the beginning, you will use your dog's name to get his attention, and that will be the indicator for the Weimaraner to look at you for what to do next.

The following list provides some name-recognition suggestions:

1. Get some treats and show one to your dog.
2. Say the dog's name and immediately say, "Yes." (Your dog should be looking at you when you speak.) Then give your dog a treat.
3. Wait 10 seconds, then show your dog a treat and repeat step two.

Sessions shouldn't last longer than about five minutes because your dog will lose focus or interest. Name recognition is something you can do several times each day. After you have done this for five to 10 sessions, the training will change a bit:
4. Wait until your dog isn't paying attention to you.
5. Call your dog. If he has a leash on, give it a gentle tug to get your dog's attention.
6. Say, "Yes," and give the dog a treat when he looks at you.

During this time, do not speak your dog's name when you correct him or for any reason other than name recognition. This is because, in the beginning, you need to get the dog to associate his name only with something positive, like treats. This will more quickly program your dog to listen to you no matter what else is going on around him.

It is likely that your Weimaraner will not require a lot of time before he recognizes his name. Repetition while looking at your pup is a great way to speed up the learning process.

Essential Commands

There are seven basic commands that all dogs should know (Sit, Down, Stay, Come, Leave It, Drop It, and Heel). These commands are the basis for a happy and enjoyable relationship with your dog, as well as giving you a way to keep your dog safe and out of trouble. Then, there are some commands that are incredibly helpful, like "Off" if you don't want pets on the furniture and "Quiet" for a noisy dog.

Train your puppy to do the commands in the order they appear in this chapter. The last two commands are optional since you may allow your dog to be on the furniture, and you may not mind a vocal canine. Since dogs sit often, "Sit" is the easiest command to teach, making it the best starting point. Teaching "Leave It" and "Drop It" is much more difficult and usually requires the puppy to fight an instinct or a desire. Consider how often you give in to something you want, even when you know you shouldn't! That's pretty much what your puppy is facing.

"Quiet" can be another difficult command, as dogs (particularly puppies) tend to bark in response to their surroundings. Some puppies do grow out of the constantly barking stage. If you finish all the other commands and find that your dog is still a bit too noisy for your home, you can then start training him to be quiet, though you will need to determine just when you want him to be quiet and when you want him to bark (like when someone is outside your home). This will take some consideration on your part.

The following are some basic steps to use during training:

1. Include everyone in the home in the Weimaraner training. The puppy must learn to listen to everyone in the household and not just one or two people. A set training schedule may only involve a couple of people in the beginning, especially if you have children. There should always be an adult present when training, but including a child will help reinforce the idea that the puppy must listen to everyone in the house. It is also an effective way for a parent to monitor a child's interaction with the puppy so that everyone plays in a way that is safe and follows the rules.
2. To get started, select an area where you and your puppy have no other distractions, including noise. Leave your phone and other devices out of range so that you are able to keep your attention on the puppy.
3. Stay happy and excited about the training. Your puppy will pick up on your enthusiasm and will focus better because of it.
4. Be consistent and firm as you teach.
5. Bring special treats to the first few training sessions, such as pieces of chicken or small treats.

Sit

Start to teach the command "Sit" when your puppy is around eight weeks old.

Once you settle into your quiet training location:
1. Hold out a treat.

2. Move the treat over your puppy's head. This will make the puppy move back.
3. Say, "Sit," as the puppy's haunches touch the floor.

Having a second person around to demonstrate this with your puppy will be helpful, as the person can sit to show the dog what you mean.

Wait until your puppy starts to sit down and say, "Sit" as he sits. If your puppy finishes sitting down, give praise. Naturally, this will make your puppy excited and wiggly, so it may take a bit of time before he will want to sit again. When your puppy calms down, repeat the process.

It's going to take more than a couple of sessions for the puppy to fully connect your words with actions. Commands are something completely new to your little companion. Once your puppy has demonstrated mastery of the command "Sit," start teaching "Down."

Down

Repeat the same process when teaching this command as you did for Sit:
1. Tell your dog to Sit.
2. Hold out the treat.
3. Lower the treat to the floor with your dog sniffing at it. Allow your pup to lick the treat, but if he stands up, start over.
4. Say "Down" as the puppy's elbows touch the floor (make sure to say it as he does the action to help him associate the word with the action), then give praise while rewarding your puppy with the treat.

It will probably take a little less time to teach this command. Wait until your puppy has mastered "Down" before moving on to "Stay."

Stay

"Stay" is a vital command to teach because it can keep your puppy from running across a street or from running at someone who is nervous or scared of dogs. It is important your dog has mastered Sit and Down before you teach Stay. Learning this command is going to be more difficult since it is not something your puppy does naturally.

Be prepared for this command to take a bit longer to teach:
1. Tell your puppy to either Sit or Stay.
2. As you do this, place your hand in front of the puppy's face.
3. Wait until the puppy stops trying to lick your hand before you continue.
4. When the puppy settles down, take a step away. If your puppy is not moving, say, "Stay," and give a treat and some praise.

Giving your puppy the reward indicates the command is over, but you also need to indicate the command is complete. The puppy has to learn to stay until you say it is okay to leave the spot. Once you give the okay to move, do not give treats. The command "Come" should not be used as the okay word, as it is a command used for something else.

Repeat these steps, taking more steps farther away from the puppy after a successful command.

Once your puppy understands Stay when you move away, start training him to stay even if you are not moving. Extend the amount of time required for the puppy to stay in one spot so that he understands Stay ends with the "Okay" command.

When you feel that your puppy has Stay mastered, start training the puppy to "Come."

Come

This is a command you can't teach until the puppy has learned the previous commands. Before you start the training session, decide if you want to use "Come" or "Come Here." Be consistent in the words you use.

This command is important for the same reason as the previous one; if you are around people who are nervous around dogs, or if you encounter a wild animal or other distraction, this command will snap your puppy's attention back to you:

1. Leash the puppy.
2. Tell the puppy to Stay.
3. Move away from the puppy.
4. Say the command you will use for Come, and give a gentle tug on the leash toward you.

Repeat these steps, building a larger distance between you and the puppy. Once the puppy seems to understand, remove the leash, and start at a close distance. If your puppy doesn't seem to understand the command, give some visual clues about what you want. For example, you can pat your leg or snap your fingers. As soon as your puppy comes running over to you, offer a reward.

Leave It

This is a difficult training command, but you need to train your dog to "Leave It" for when you are out on a walk and want him to ignore other people or dogs.

1. Let your dog see that you have treats in your hand, then close your hand. Your fist should be close enough for your dog to sniff the treat.
2. Say, "Leave it," when your dog starts to sniff your hand.
3. Say, "Yes," and give your dog a treat when he turns his head away from the treats. Initially, this will probably take a while, as your dog will want those treats. Don't continue to say "Leave it," as your dog should not be learning that you will give a command more than once. You want him to learn he must do what you say the first time, which is why treats are recommended in the beginning. If a minute or more passes after giving the command, you can then issue it again, but make sure your canine is focused on you and not distracted.

These sessions should only last about five minutes. Your dog will need time to learn this command as you are teaching him to ignore something he naturally wants. When he looks away and stops sniffing when you say, "Leave it," you can move on to more advanced versions of the training:

1. Leave your hand open so that your dog can see the treats.
2. Say, "Leave it," when your dog starts to show interest. This will probably be immediate since your hand will be open, so be prepared.
   A. Close your fist if your dog continues to sniff or gets near the treats in your hand.
   B. Give your dog a treat from your other hand if he stops.

Repeat these steps until your dog finally stops trying to sniff the treats. When your dog seems to have learned this command, move on to the most difficult version of this command.

1. Place treats on the ground, or let your dog see you hide them. Then stay close to those treats.
2. Say "Leave it" when your dog starts to show interest in sniffing the treats.
   A. Place a hand over the treats if he doesn't listen.
   B. Give a treat if your dog does listen.

From here, you can start training while standing farther from the treat with your dog leashed so you can stop him if needed. Then start to use other things that your dog loves, such as a favorite toy or another tempting treat that you don't usually give him.

Drop It

This is going to be one of the most difficult commands to teach because it goes against both your puppy's instincts and interests. Your puppy wants to keep whatever he has, so you are going to have to offer him something better instead. It is essential to teach the command early, as your Weimaraner could be very destructive in the early days. Furthermore, this command could save your pooch's life. When you are out for a walk, he will probably lunge at objects that look like food. However, once he has mastered this command, he will drop anything he picks up.

Start with a toy and a large treat that your dog cannot eat in a matter of seconds, such as a rawhide. Make sure the treat you have is one your puppy does not get very often so that there is motivation to drop the toy or big treat.

1. Give your puppy the toy or large treat. If you want to use a clicker, too, pair it with the exciting treat you will use to help convince your puppy to drop the treat.
2. Show your puppy the exciting treat.
3. Say, "Drop it," and when he drops the treat or toy, tell him, "Good," and hand over the exciting treat while picking up the dropped item.
4. Repeat this immediately after your puppy finishes eating the exciting treat.

You will need to keep reinforcing this command for months after it is learned because it is not a natural instinct.

Heel

"Heel" is a command that is incredibly beneficial. It keeps your dog from weaving in front of you on a walk, potentially being a tripping hazard, and gives you a command that will help to distract your dog if a squirrel or other small animal crosses your path. Telling your dog to "heel" if you see the squirrel first can be a good reminder to your dog not to chase the squirrel.

Equally important, "heel" is a command that you need to use when socializing your dog. Your Weimaraner should know how to heel before you really start socializing him to ensure that your dog is calmer or at least is still listening to you when you approach other people and dogs.

The purpose of this command is to teach your dog to walk by your side. This can be incredibly frustrating and annoying in practice, which is what really leads to people failing to teach this command. When we go outside, we get distracted, or we just want to hurry and get back inside—especially if it is cold, hot, or raining. Failing to be consistent with this command will undermine your efforts to actually teach it. Training in all of the other commands will help you to learn your dog's personality, what works, and the rewards that will keep your Weimaraner's attention during training to "heel."

Have some of your dog's favorite treats in a small bag that you can quickly and easily access. Cut the treats down to a small size (about the size of a penny) because you are going to be giving a lot of these in the early days.

Training will begin inside. This means you will probably want to leash your dog inside, which can lead to excitement if your dog thinks you are going outside. If that happens, calm your dog before you start training. Choose the room with the most space for walking around; halls can be a good choice since there is typically ample room for walking in a straight line, which will be more like walking outside.

1. Determine which side you want your dog to walk on, then hold a treat up to your chest on the side where you want the dog so that your dog cannot reach it. This will help will your dog focus on listening to your commands. The side you choose should be the side where you want your dog to walk when you go outside; usually, people train dogs to walk on their left side; but choose the side that is most comfortable for you.
2. Point to the side you prefer and call the dog's name, then say the word "Heel."
3. Give your puppy a treat as soon as he reaches the correct side and say "yes" or "good." If you also plan to use a clicker, use it as you give your dog the treat. Having the treat on the same side as your dog will keep him from crossing to the wrong side.
4. Move away from your dog, point to the same side, call his name and say, "Heel."
5. Immediately reward him for coming and standing on the correct side.

Over the next few days, as your dog starts to understand what you want him to do without treats, you can start trying to throw him off by zigzagging or turning to teach him to keep you as a point of reference. When he gets the concept and remains on the correct side, start getting his attention by saying, "Look," and making eye contact. This reinforces that his attention needs to be on you and on staying by your side.

Once your dog is able to do this inside, you can start working on Heel when you are outside. You want to make sure that your dog understands the command before going outside, where there are so many distractions. If your dog is accustomed to being on one side when walking, it will be more automatic for your dog, which will go a long way toward helping your dog stay focused when you move from the controlled home environment to the more chaotic outdoors.

You will need to keep reinforcing this command for months after it is learned because it is not a natural instinct.

Off

This is different from training your dog not to jump on people (Chapter 9). This command is specifically to get your dog off furniture or surfaces that may be dangerous. If your furniture has enough space for your dog, you may not need to train for this one until a bit later. Master the other commands first, then start on this one as practice for when you and your dog go somewhere else and you need him to refrain from using other people's furniture.

This is training you will need to do on the fly because you are training your dog to stop an action. This means you have to react to that undesirable action. Having treats on hand will be essential when you see your dog getting up on things you don't want him to be on:

1. Wait for your dog to put his paws on something you don't want him on.
2. Say, "Off," and lure him away with a treat that you keep just out of his reach.
3. Say, "Yes," and give him a treat as soon as his paws are off the surface.

Repeat this every time you see the behavior. It will probably take at least half a dozen times before your dog understands he should not perform the action anymore. Over time, switch from treats to praise or playing with a toy.

Quiet

This is one of those fewer large dogs that can get pretty vocal if you don't teach them to tone down that need to bark. Initially, you can use treats sparingly to reinforce quiet if your pup enjoys making noise:

1. When your puppy barks for no obvious reason, tell him to be quiet and place a treat nearby. It is almost guaranteed your dog will fall silent to sniff the treat.
2. If your dog does fall silent, say, "Good dog" or "Good quiet."

Where to Go from Here

Weimaraners can definitely benefit from classes, even if you are a great trainer. For them, getting to see other dogs and learning to listen can be sped up when done in different types of environments. Most dogs will need some additional training so that you can keep them from being overexuberant and reckless. When you have a large breed like the Weimaraner, getting your dog trained quickly without getting upset or frustrated may require that you get outside help. Puppies get big incredibly quickly, and adult dogs are going to be difficult to train if they don't have much experience with training. Chapter 13 provides alternatives for helping your dog use up all of his energy, but you need to at least ensure that your dog learns the basic commands. The following classes can help you learn to keep yourself calm so that your training is effective. These classes are really as much for you as for your dog.

Puppy Classes

> *A puppy class is a great beginning for introducing your Weimaraner puppy to other dogs. We've attended both private training classes and those offered by pet stores, and sometimes, vet offices, and all were valuable. Of course, some trainers are more knowledgeable and experienced than others. You can elicit help with problems and help others with your successes. It will at least expose your puppy to other sizes and temperaments of dogs in a safe, controlled environment, and besides that, it's just FUN!*
>
> KYRA SCHLIEMAN
> *SilverLining Weimaraners*

Puppies can begin to go to puppy school as early as six weeks, but you will probably want to wait until your Weimaraner has had all of his shots. You will need to set aside an hour or two so that you can research schools near you. Make sure to take the time to read the reviews and see if you can talk to people who have used a particular school or trainer. Trainers should be willing to take the time to talk to you and answer questions as well, so try talking to the people running the school. This is the beginning of obedience training, but you need to be careful around other dogs until your puppy has completed his vaccinations. Talk with your vet about when is an appropriate time to begin classes. Your vet may also be able to recommend good puppy training classes in your area.

The primary purpose of these classes is socialization. Studies show one-third of all puppies have minimal exposure to unfamiliar people and dogs during the first 20 weeks of their life. This can make the outside world pretty scary! The puppy classes give you and your puppy a chance to learn how to meet and greet other people and dogs in a controlled environment. Dogs that attend these classes are much friendlier and are less stressed about such things as large trucks, thunder, loud noises, and unfamiliar visitors. They are also less likely to be nervous or suffer from separation anxiety, a likely issue for a Weimaraner.

Puppy classes are also great training for you! The same studies show owners who attend classes learn to react appropriately when a puppy is disobedient or misbehaves. The classes teach you how to train your puppy and how to deal with the emerging headstrong nature of your dog.

Many classes will help you with some of the basic commands, like Sit and Down. Look for a class that also focuses on socialization so that your puppy can get the most out of the instruction.

Obedience Training

After your puppy graduates from puppy school and understands most of the basic commands, you can switch to obedience classes. Some trainers offer at-home obedience training, but if you do this, it's still a good idea to also set aside regular time to socialize your pup at a dog park. If your Weimaraner attends puppy classes, the trainers there can recommend classes at the next level of training. Dogs of nearly any age can attend obedience training classes, although your dog should be old enough to listen to commands before instruction begins.

Obedience training usually includes the following:
- Teaching or reinforcing basic commands, like Sit, Stay, Come, and Down
- How to walk without pulling on the leash
- How to properly greet people and dogs, including not jumping on them

Obedience school is as much about training you as training your dog. It helps you learn how to train your puppy while teaching your dog basic commands and how to behave for basic tasks, like greetings and walking. Classes usually last between seven and 10 weeks.

Ask your vet for recommendations and also consider the following when evaluating trainers:
- Are they certified, particularly the CPDT-KA certification?
- How many years have they been training dogs?
- Do they have experience with training Weimaraners?

Can you participate in the training? If the answer is no, do not use that trainer. You have to be a part of your dog's training because the trainer won't be around for most of your dog's life. Therefore, your dog has to learn to listen to you.

If your dog has anxiety, depression, or other serious behavioral problems, you need to hire a trainer to help your dog work through those issues. Do your research to be sure your trainer is an expert—preferably one with experience training intelligent, strong-willed dogs.

Once your Weimaraner understands the basic commands and has done well in obedience training, you will know if more difficult training is right for him.

CHAPTER 12

Socialization

That friendly gregarious reputation is based on a dog that tends to be a lover, but the fact that they have a long history of hunting shouldn't be ignored , so fighting isn't entirely absent in their history. Fortunately, that affable nature is going to make socialization easy. However, you do need a controlled environment because these puppies may be a bit on the hyper side, which can be upsetting to other dogs.

Breeders tend to spend a good bit of time socializing their Weimaraner puppies, so they should have a fairly good baseline when they arrive at your house. A lot of breeders strongly recommend that puppies be taken to obedience training, not just for the training but the socialization.

Weimaraner puppies can be easy to socialize because they haven't quite learned to be wary of other dogs and people. They are excited about meeting others, making this the best stage to start socializing them. You will always need to ensure that they are well-behaved when meeting others because it is far too easy for a Weimaraner puppy to be overenthusiastic, something that can get dangerous when they get to be a larger size. They do have some protective instincts after they become adults, so socialization is essential. By nature, they want to have fun, especially if everyone is feeling good.

With a large breed, you are going to be more limited in where you can socialize your dog. Until your dog is comfortable out in public, you want to

CELEBRITY WEIMARANER
Weimaraner in the White House

President Dwight D. Eisenhower, 34th president of the United States from 1953 to 1961, owned a Weimar-aner named Heidi. This beloved pet lived at the White House with the Eisenhowers for several years be-fore retiring to the Eisenhower farm in Gettysburg, where she had a litter of puppies.

Chapter 12: Socialization

make sure to keep interactions limited to a controlled environment—at least as controlled as it can be out in public.

Another benefit of early socialization is that it can make life much more enjoyable for everyone involved, no matter what the situation. A socialized dog will approach the world from a much better place than a dog that is not socialized.

Greeting New People

> *As soon as the puppy has had the appropriate shots, start walking in your neighborhood. When it's old enough, start puppy training classes. Have your dog-friendly friends and their children over to play with your puppy and bring their dog-friendly pets! Make sure you know their dogs are good with puppies.*
>
> CHRISTINE GRISELL
> *Nani's Weimaraners*

Puppies will likely enjoy meeting new people, so make sure to invite friends over to help socialize your new canine family member. Your Weimaraner may initially react by barking, but this likely will stop as soon as the person tries to pet your pooch. Still, you will need to be careful to make sure that there are no territorial behaviors.

The following is a list of methods to use when introducing your puppy to a new person:

- Try to have your puppy meet new people daily, if possible. This could be during walks or while you are doing other activities, both inside and outside of the house. If you can't meet new people daily, try to do so at least four times a week.
- Invite friends and family over and let them spend a few minutes giving the puppy their undivided attention. If your puppy has a favorite game or activity, let people know so they can play with him. This will win the little guy over very quickly and teach him new people are fun and safe to be around.
- Once your puppy is old enough to learn to do tricks (after the first month), have your new friend perform his tricks for visitors.
- Avoid crowds for the first few months. When your puppy is older, attend dog-friendly events so your pup can learn to be comfortable around a large group of people.

Greeting New Dogs

> *Only socialize your Weim with known, friendly dogs that tolerate puppies and that are more homebody types, not weekend warriors at dog parks or day cares. Wait until they have had all the vaccines and even then, be mindful of exposure to viruses like Parvo.*
>
> JESSICA HANSON
> *Hanson Weimaraners*

Chapter 12: Socialization

Photo Courtesy of Amanda Unger

Chapter 8 explained how to introduce your new Weimaraner to your other dogs. However, meeting dogs that are not part of your household is a little different, especially since you may encounter them at any time when you are out walking. The goal is to be able to walk around your neighborhood and have your dog remain calm, refraining from running up to other dogs that may not be as friendly. The problem will likely be with the other dog. If the other dog is not sociable, having another pup running toward it may be upsetting. Therefore, you need to train your Weimaraner as early as possible to keep him safe.

Most dogs will bow and sniff each other during an introduction. Remember to watch for signs of aggression (Chapter 8), such as raised hackles and bared teeth. It is unlikely, but it is best to be safe. Bowing, high tail, and perked ears usually mean that your Weimaraner is excited about meeting the other dog. If your Weimaraner is making noises, make sure that the sounds are playful by paying attention to the physical reaction. This applies more if you have adopted an adult than if you have a puppy, but it is always a good idea to keep an eye out for these signs, regardless of the age of your dog.

The best way to help a Weimaraner feel comfortable around unfamiliar dogs is to set up playdates with other dogs in a neutral place. This should make the whole experience much easier. If you have friends with dogs that are known to be very friendly, see if they are willing to meet up to have your dogs meet and play.

Don't let your Weimaraner jump up on other dogs, no matter how excited he is. This action can become a way of showing dominance, which you really don't want with your puppy, even if it is just play in the beginning. If he does jump up, immediately say, "No," to let him know it is not acceptable behavior.

The Importance of Continuing Socialization

Even friendly dogs need socialization. When family and friends visit, encourage them to bring their dogs. This will remind your Weimaraner his home is a welcoming place and not somewhere he needs to exert his dominance. You do not want your pup to think he can be a terror in his own house.

You will want to do some of the early activities with your puppy fairly early in your dog's life so that he has exposure to a wider range of environments, sounds, smells, and experiences. If you want to bike with your dog, expose your dog to bikes so that the bike becomes a normal item. You won't be able to run with your Weimaraner quite yet, but you can take him to new places where he can get an idea of what those places are like. The familiarization of new locations and the kinds of things that are in those areas will help your dog feel comfortable as he moves into maturity.

Socializing an Adult Dog

> *Some Weims love to socialize and some do not ... Most Weims are social and love to romp with others, but they can be protective of you, so it's best to take them to a 'new' place off-lead when meeting new playmates.*
>
> **TONI FOW**
> *Wing It Weimaraners*

Chapter 12: Socialization

Socializing an adult canine requires a lot of time, dedication, gentle training, and a firm approach. There's no guarantee that your dog will be happy being around other dogs. You may be lucky enough to get an adult that is already well-socialized. That does not mean you can remain entirely relaxed! Your new dog may have had a terrible experience with a particular breed of dog that no one knows about, and this can result in a bad situation.

Photo Courtesy of Charles Rudziewicz

Your dog should be adept at the following commands before you work on socialization:
- Sit
- Down
- Stay
- Heel

"Heel" and "Stay" are especially important because they demonstrate that your dog has self-control by remaining in one place based on your command. This quality will be helpful when socializing because using this command will allow you to control your Weimaraner in any situation. When you go outside, you will need to be very aware of your surroundings and be able to command your dog before another dog or person gets near you.

- Use a short leash on walks. Being aware of your surroundings will start to cue you in to what is making your dog react so that you can start training him not to react negatively.
- Change direction if you notice your Weimaraner is not reacting well to a person or dog that is approaching. Avoidance is a good

short-term solution until you know your dog is more accepting of the presence of other dogs or people.
- If you are not able to take a different direction, tell your dog to sit, then block his view. This can prove to be particularly challenging, as he will try to look around from behind you. Continue to distract your dog so he will listen to you, taking his mind off what is coming toward him.
- Ask friends with friendly dogs to visit you, then meet in an enclosed space. Having one or two friendly dogs to interact with can help your Weimaraner realize not all dogs are dangerous or need to be put in their place. When dogs wander around the area together, with no real interaction, your dog will learn that the others are enjoying the outside too. So, there is no reason to try to bully them!
- Get special treats for when you go walking. If your dog is aggressive when walking, have him sit and give him one of the special

treats. Weimaraners are food motivated, so this could be a perfect way of distracting your dog from whatever is making him feel protective. At the first snarl or sign of aggression, engage the training mentality and draw upon your dog's desire for those special treats. This method is slow, but it is reliable because your dog will learn that the appearance of strangers and other dogs means special treats for him. He will realize going on a walk is a positive experience, not a negative one. Nonetheless, this does not train him to interact with those dogs. Combine this tip with the previous suggestion to get the best results.

If you have ongoing problems with your adult dog, consult a behaviorist or specialized trainer. It might be that you should keep your dog home all of the time, in which case you are going to need a big yard to ensure your dog stays healthy. It's never worth the risk of having your Weimaraner around other dogs if your dog doesn't like his peers. An expert may be able to help you so that you and your dog don't have to live a more hermit-like lifestyle.

CHAPTER 13

Playtime and Exercise

This is the reason why people get Weimaraners – there is so much you can do with them because they have the energy and interest to be active. When you feel like trying something new, your Weimaraner is going to be game. When you want to settle into a comfortable exercise schedule, your Weimaraner can help you stick to it. Weimaraners are one of the best workout companions, as well as being fantastic all-around activity participants. This is a breed that is prone to overeating, which is always bad, but it shouldn't be too much of a problem if you keep your dog active.

Pretty much from the beginning, Weimaraners will keep you busy, but you have to be very careful of their growing bones. Adult Weimaraners are essentially creatures of boundless energy that are up for whatever activity you throw at them.

Weimaraners love all kinds of activities—swimming, hiking, long walks, exploring trails, or sniffing along the beach. Pretty much anything you can name that is active but doesn't require equipment, your Weimaraner is likely to be willing to join you. And you don't have to worry too much about moving too fast for them. This is a breed that can do almost anything you do and will happily keep up with whatever challenges you present. When your active day is over, they make fantastic cuddle buddies as you relax. Conversely, when you own a Weimaraner, you also really can't afford to take a day off from exercising because your dog is absolutely going to need daily activity. That isn't going to be difficult if you have a sizable yard where your dog can romp with you on days you don't want to go anywhere.

Chapter 13: Playtime and Exercise

There are a number of positives for your dog when you ensure he gets regular exercise sessions.
- It helps keep your dog at a healthier weight.
- He will be tired enough not to be too much trouble, especially if you need to leave him alone for a little while.
- Exercise is a great time to bond with your Weimaraner.

Exercise Needs

> *Weims thrive in active households where they get plenty of physical and mental activity. Ideally, the home has access to an area where the Weim can free run, use its nose, explore natural areas, and interact with the environment.*
>
> **ANNE TYSON**
> *Regen Weimaraners*

Weimaraners need at least an hour of vigorous daily exercise until they reach their senior years (Chapter 18). Aim for a 30-minute activity in the morning and another 30-minute round of activities in the evening. On weekends and vacation days, you can spend a lot more time out of doors having fun. If your Weimaraner is not getting enough activity, it will probably be very obvious. He will take out his energy and boredom on your furniture, doors, and home when he is still young. When he is a mature adult, it will not be so obvious unless you are checking his weight regularly. It can get dangerous if you don't meet a Weimaraner's exercise needs because being overweight will increase the potential for a lot of ailments, especially as your dog ages.

If you have a puppy, frequent 10-to-15-minute training sessions can be the activity as well. Short walks can double as training sessions. You can try "Sit" and "Heel" during walks once your dog reaches a stage where he is able to do these commands well in your home.

You will definitely have limits about how much cold and rainy weather you can handle. This doesn't mean that your Weimaraner can skip being active—not if you don't want your dog to take it out around your home.

Chapter 13: Playtime and Exercise

Fortunately, there are plenty of indoor activities that you can do on days when going outside really isn't such a good idea.

Outdoor Activities

The possibilities are pretty much endless in terms of what your Weimaraner can do outside. If you live in an area with snow, he will be the perfect companion for kids playing in the snow or going out to do chores and other activities in the cold. If you live near woods, your Weimaraner will love exploring and hiking around the area. If you live in a city or suburban area, your Weimaraner can join you for jogs and bike rides. If you want to be outside, you have a dog who can join you for pretty much everything except rock climbing.

Agility Training

If you want to train your Weimaraner for this one, it is an activity that will tire your dog out both physically and mentally. At the end of a session of agility training, you may have a few minutes of downtime where your Weimaraner will be happy to be lazy while he is recharging.

This is an activity that really helps you bond with your Weimaraner, and if you enjoy it, you and your dog will have a great outlet for engaging in an activity that reliably tires your dog. Agility training includes a lot of different items, including

HELPFUL TIP

Considering Dog Sports

Weimaraners were originally bred as hunting dogs for a German grand duke and his noblemen in the Court of Weimar. Initially bred to hunt large game, such as wolves and boar, these dogs still have astonishing stamina. Today, there are a plethora of dog sports available to the public. Agility, tracking, and obstacle courses are all excellent options for Weimaraners. In addition, swimming is a great choice because it's easy on your Weimaraner's joints and helps him expend plenty of energy. Many owners claim that their Weimaraners start to settle down between the ages of three and five years old.

tunnels, hurdles, cones, teeter-totters, and ramps. You can focus on the activities that your dog really seems to love over time, but you'll want to keep changing up the course because that is what keeps your dog having to think about how best to get through it. The courses should not be predictable to get the most out of each session.

Before beginning, you need to take your Weimaraner to the vet to make sure he is alright. This means a complete regular checkup. Agility training consumes a lot of stamina and works the dog's body in a way that could do harm if they aren't in good enough shape to get started.

To start, there are a number of agility training clubs that can introduce you and your dog to the sport. You can see what kinds of courses they have, learn about recommendations, and see other dogs in action. Over time, you may be able to create your own course at home (you will need a larger yard for this), then you won't need to travel to run through this fun activity. Still, you should probably continue with the club as a way of having some variety with your dog – this will help to keep the sport fun for both you and the dog. It is also a great way to have some built in socialization time with your Weimaraner.

Course Training

Also known as Lure coursing, this has your dog chase after something moving quickly. Since Weimaraners started as hunters, this gives them some outlet for doing what comes naturally to them – chasing. Unlike hunting through, the lures aren't animals, just fake items that look realistic and move on a mechanism to stay ahead of the dogs. The lures are able to quickly change direction, giving the dogs a real run for their money as it isn't just running in a straight line. This is what makes this particularly challenging – your Weimaraner has to stay on his toes to chase the lure, which will clearly tire him out by the end of the run.

Like agility training, your dog needs to go to the vet to ensure a clean bill of health to get started. You can probably find some lure clubs in your area. Unlike coursing, you really can't do this one at home because it requires a lot of room for running and some more complicated mechanisms. However, it does provide a great way to get out and socialize your Weimaraner regularly.

Advanced Training

Weimaraners are incredibly agile, so they can play a wide range of sports, like tracking, flyball, and water sports. All of these require additional training specific to the sport, but if you find you want to branch out beyond the other activities, the possibilities for a large, energetic, intelligent breed like the Weimaraner are pretty much endless.

An Avid Swimmer

Weimaraners only have one short coat and that doesn't interfere with swimming. Also, they have webbed feet. This is a dog that can keep up with you in the pool or a natural body of water. However, they do need to be introduced to swimming early in life.

Start your Weimaraner in pools, ponds, and smaller lakes. Shallower depths can help your dog feel safer faster. Don't worry—you don't have to teach your dog to swim. Any initial apprehension will give way to those well-honed instincts, and your dog will be swimming much faster than any human, usually by the end of the first swim. Still, keep going to the shallower locations for at least the first few swims.

Once your dog is happy and excited about water, you can move on to deeper water. Just make sure that you stay close and always keep an eye on your dog. Your Weimaraner may overdo swimming in the beginning, then not have enough energy to return. If you go to an ocean or other large body of water, consider a life vest for your dog but also remain vigilant.

Hiking and Backpacking

> *Retrieving tennis balls with the ball launchers when the dog is older can be excellent exercise; it really gives them a workout and is easy to do. Obviously hiking, long walks, running, or biking (are all great) when (your Weim is) mature, orthopedically sound, and the exercise is okayed by your vet.*
>
> **KYRA SCHLIEMAN**
> *SilverLining Weimaraners*

If you love being out in nature, this is a great dog to take hiking and backpacking. Weimaraners can easily keep up with you, and they will enjoy the sights as much as you (and the smells a lot more). They are made for being out and getting time in the woods, mountains, and forests, making them the ideal companions for outdoor enthusiasts.

Frisbee

Since teeth issues are a potential problem for Weimaraners, you will want to use something soft for this game. There are plenty of great discs

Chapter 13: Playtime and Exercise

you can use that won't harm your dog's mouth. A soft disc usually runs between $5 and $20, so it won't be a major investment.

All you have to do is throw the disc, and your dog will get it. Training your dog to bring it back is going to be the trick, but given how much fun this game is likely to be with your dog, this shouldn't be too hard. Just add "Fetch" to your training, and your dog will be more than happy with the results.

Keep in mind this is a very drooly dog, so it won't take long before those discs are slimy when

Photo Courtesy of Annabella Alfaro

you play. Also, those big teeth are probably going to do some damage to the discs. If your dog enjoys the game, it won't hurt to get a stash of discs so that you don't run out of them. When you play, take a couple of discs with you so that you can rotate which one you are throwing to reduce the amount of drool you have to deal with.

Treasure Hunting

> The best exercise for a Weim is hunting. If the home isn't a hunting home, then allowing the pup access to a safe, open area to explore off leash often satisfies a Weim's need to explore and use its nose.
>
> ANNE TYSON
> Regen Weimaraners

Photo Courtesy of Stacey Perez

Weimaraners have a lot of skills, and you can really encourage your dog to explore those skills by conducting treasure hunts. In addition to tiring out your canine, these can help keep him feeling mentally stimulated and happy. The fact that it means getting a bit more praise will be the icing on the cake as far as your dog is concerned.

1. Establish what you want the treasure to be. It should be something that your dog doesn't get often. Treats are usually the go-to because they provide something with a smell he will want. You can buy something special, or you can make a treat to really get your dog excited.

2. For the first round, let your dog watch you hide the treat. This is how you introduce your dog to the idea of you putting something out of sight and that you want him going to retrieve it. You will probably need to do this several times, so if you use treats, give him smaller pieces instead of a full, large treat during the learning process. Change where you "hide" the treat so that your dog understands that it isn't always in the same place.
3. When you feel that your dog gets what you want him to do, tell your good boy to "Stay" (or if you haven't gotten that far in training, have someone hold your dog), then go hide the treat someplace where your dog can't see you hiding it. Over time, you can actually hide treats in multiple locations to really challenge your dog's abilities to sniff out where the treats are. Return to your dog and let him go hunting. When he finds a treat, be effusive in your praise to let him know he's doing it right.

A treat with a lot of praise? Yeah, this can easily be one of your dog's favorite games really quickly. It's also something you can play inside, though you may want to use dry treats instead of something that could get ground into your furniture, carpet, or other items.

Traveling

> *Weims are generally great travelers. The safest way to travel with any dog is in a crate. Bring a leash, water, a dish, food, and a clean-up kit. Try to find a safe place to allow the dog to get some off-leash exercise. If that isn't possible, then walks where it is allowed to sniff and use its nose will help the dog settle for a long trip.*
>
> ANNE TYSON
> *Regen Weimaraners*

A well-trained and well-socialized Weimaraner can be one of the best travel companions because he will love being wherever you are. Flying is a really bad idea because they do not do well at high altitudes. What you need is a big vehicle that lets you travel at your own pace. Your Weimaraner will love to see new places, experience new smells, and will enjoy the sights and sounds of traveling and camping wherever you go.

Make sure to travel with water so that your dog doesn't get dehydrated. Considering how easily Weimaraners overheat, you'll want to ensure that the car ride is as comfortable and safe as possible. It is probably best to have your dog in a crate or secured so that he doesn't fall over during sudden stops or turns.

Build in stops for pee breaks, making sure to stop at least every four hours. This will not only give your dog a chance to sniff and enjoy a new place, but you'll have a chance to stretch your back and legs (which is really better for you too).

You will want to start traveling when your Weimaraner is young, such as taking him to the park, store, or other location. Once your canine is trained in all of the basic commands, you can go for longer trips knowing that you can keep your dog safe and secure, even when you encounter other people and dogs.

Put Them to Work

This is a breed with a working history, so it isn't too much of a stretch to start putting a Weimaraner to work, with there being a need for more dogs in therapy. With a gregarious, loving nature, a lot of Weimaraner can make for great therapy dogs. You will need to wait until your dog is a bit older and calmer before he can start to do this, but as your Weimaraner starts to slow down, working as therapy dogs can give them the kind of attention that makes up for not being as active.

This one will require a good bit of research as you will need to determine what requirements and training your dog needs prior to registering him as a therapy dog. It is possible that your dog won't be able to be a therapy dog if he can't meet the requirements. If he does, you can complete any necessary training classes, certifications, or other training, then register your dog. This will be a bit of a time dedication for you, but it will replace some of the time when you used to be incredibly active, something that may actually work better if you either have less time to be really physically active or if you are also slowing down.

Indoor Activities

The real downside to having a larger dog is that during bad weather, it is much harder to make sure he gets enough daily exercise. Here are some things you can do inside to help your dog stay healthy.

Hide-and-Seek

Hide-and-seek is a game you can play once your dog understands proper behavior in the home. Since your Weimaraner will probably hear you wherever you hide, you can also make it a game of hide the toy. If you distract your pup while someone else hides the toy, your Weimaraner will have a fun time trying to locate it!

More Training

> *Teaching your dog new tricks is mentally stimulating. Even placing a favorite bed near a window so the dog can look out during the day is stimulating ... Toys of all kinds ... some are more interested in toys than others; rotate the toys and show interest and interact with them too—hide some peanut butter or cheese in a Kong. Make your dog work for the reward!*
>
> KYRA SCHLIEMAN
> *SilverLining Weimaraners*

On gloomy or hot days, you can teach your dog nearly anything, such as roll over and play dead, to make sure he's tired at the end of the day. Remember, Weimaraners are very much a dog that wants to please, and they are intelligent enough to be able to get pretty much any command you give them. Once you run out of tricks you find online, you can start working on your own training ideas to get your dog to be a unique performer.

Puzzle Toys!

Puzzle toys are a fun way to get your dog to move around without you having to do much. Most puzzle toys are food-based, so the dog will need to figure out how to get the treats out. If you use these toys, keep in mind that your dog isn't likely to work off the extra calories consumed from puzzle treats, and you should adjust his meals accordingly.

Cuddle Time

Younger Weimaraners aren't likely to be fans of cuddling unless they are tired—just like toddlers or small children. Once they get older and settle down, these dogs can be absolutely fantastic cuddlers because they just love being around you. As long as you make sure your Weimaraner gets enough exercise, he will be just as happy to relax at the end of the day as you are.

What to Avoid

There are a lot of things you can do to exercise a Weimaraner, but with an intelligent dog like this, you have to be very careful about not letting him get into trouble. The following paragraphs are related to things you should avoid.

Overexertion in Puppies

Weimaraner puppies grow rapidly, meaning their growth plates are not closed until the dog is about 18 months old. The best way to work out the energy of a Weimaraner puppy is to give him a lot of off-leash play on soft surfaces, such as lawns. Swimming is also a great activity if you start training him early, and it won't hurt his joints.

Puppies also get tired as much by mental work as by physical activity. They don't require nearly as much activity to tire out as an adult. Let their flagging energy levels help you determine when to stop play, and be ready for them to be energetic all too soon afterward.

> *Off-leash running is always a great exercise for Weims, although puppies should be held back somewhat from excessive running until at least 15 or 16 months of age to allow for the full development of joints.*
>
> **JOE WIDOMSKI**
> *Shade of Grey Weimaraners*

Hot Weather

Chapter 15 details best grooming practices for this breed, but hot weather is always going to be problematic for Weimaraners. Avoid exercising during the heat of the day. If a dog gets too hot, he can suffer heat stress or, in the worst cases, heatstroke. The following are signs that your dog may be suffering from one of these conditions:

- Excessive panting or whining
- Sudden lethargy or confusion
- Tongue is hanging out more than usual and is shaped like a scoop at the end
- Gums and tongue appear red

It is best to keep your Weimaraner inside on hot days and do some indoor activities. If you do want to go outside to be active, do it either very early in the morning or around/after dusk.

Post Meal Exercise

> *Weims can be susceptible to bloat. It is important to limit excessive activity to an hour or so before and after eating.*
>
> **JOE WIDOMSKI**
> *Shade of Grey Weimaraners*

Unfortunately, Weimaraners are at risk of gastric dilation volvulus, better known as bloat. The ailment is covered in detail in Chapter 17, but one of the ways to increase the risk of this life-threatening problem is to exercise your dog right after eating. Give your dog at least an hour to digest his food before you do any kind of exercise; some experts recommend waiting two hours to be safe.

PART 4

Taking Care of Your Weimaraner

CHAPTER 14

Nutrition

All large dogs require a considerable amount of attention to their diet to ensure they remain healthy, have a high quality of life, and live as long as possible. Considering puppies are typically fully grown at about one year but are not considered to be adults until they are around three, it is essential to ensure your high-energy puppy has the right foods to help him grow strong and healthy.

> *All Weims are different. Find a high quality food that agrees with your Weim.*
>
> ANNE TYSON
> *Regen Weimaraners*

Even though this is a high energy dog that loves to be active, Weimaraners are also highly food motivated. Your dog is going to want to eat as often as you are willing to feed him. Between treats for training and meals, it is very easy to overfeed Weimaraners, which can be detrimental to their health. Maintaining their sleek bodies is essential to the breed being healthy, so when they are overweight, it increases the risk for a lot of potential ailments that are otherwise easy to avoid.

Why a Healthy Diet is Important

HEALTH ALERT!
A Healthy Weight

Despite their high energy levels, Weimaraners are not immune to obesity. A lack of exercise, poor diet, or other medical issues can cause unhealthy weight gain. Weimaraners are extremely high-energy dogs and require an average of two or more hours of exercise daily. If this exercise goal isn't met, your dog may be-come lethargic or depressed, leading to weight gain. If you have any concerns about your Weimaraner's weight, don't hesitate to speak with your veterinarian and rule out any underlying medical conditions.

Since they are so large, Weimaraners need more calories to sustain themselves. However, you probably aren't going to need to worry about your dog getting enough food—this is a breed that is incredibly food driven. Even if your Weimaraner is active, it doesn't mean he is burning all the calories he takes in, especially if you have an open treat policy. Just as you should not be eating all day, your puppy shouldn't be either. If you have a busy schedule, it will be too easy for your dog to have substantial lapses in activity levels while you are not ensuring he gets the recommended daily exercise (covered in Chapter 13).

You need to be aware of roughly how many calories your dog eats a day, including treats, so be mindful of your dog's weight and whether or not he is putting on pounds. This will tell you if you should adjust his food intake or if you should change the food to something more nutritious but with fewer calories.

Always talk with your vet if you have concerns about your Weimaraner's weight.

Dangerous Foods

Dogs can eat some raw meat without having to worry about the kinds of problems a person would encounter. However, there are some human foods that could be fatal to your Weimaraner, in part because the kinds of raw meat that humans offer have been treated with a range of chemicals. Raw diets will be examined later in this chapter so you can protect your Weimaraner from the potential risks associated with raw foods.

The following is a list of foods you should **NEVER** feed your dog:
- Apple seeds
- Chocolate
- Coffee
- Cooked bones (They can kill a dog when the bones splinter in the dog's mouth or stomach.)
- Corn on the cob (The cob is deadly to dogs; corn off the cob is fine.)
- Grapes/raisins
- Macadamia nuts
- Onions and chives
- Peaches, persimmons, and plums
- Tobacco (Your Weimaraner will not realize it is not a food and may eat it if it's left out.)
- Xylitol (a sugar substitute in candies and baked goods)
- Yeast

In addition to this list, consult the Canine Journal for a lengthy list of other dangerous foods. (http://www.caninejournal.com/foods-not-to-feed-dog/)

Canine Nutrition

Canines are largely carnivorous, and protein is a significant dietary need (as discussed later in this chapter). However, they need more than just protein to be healthy.

Chapter 14: Nutrition

The following table provides the primary nutritional requirements for dogs:

Nutrient	Sources	Puppy	Adult
Protein	Meat, eggs, soybeans, corn, wheat, peanut butter	22.0% of diet	18.0% of diet
Fats	Fish oil, flaxseed oil, canola oil, pork fat, poultry fat, safflower oil, sunflower oil, soybean oil	8.0 to 15.0% of diet	5.0 to 15.0% of diet
Calcium	Dairy, animal organ tissue, meats, legumes (typically beans)	1.0% of diet	0.6% of diet
Phosphorus	Meat and pet supplements	0.8% of diet	0.5% of diet
Sodium	Meat, eggs	0.3% of diet	0.06% of diet

The following are the remaining nutrients dogs require, all of them less than 1% of a puppy or adult diet:
- Arginine
- Histidine
- Isoleucine
- Leucine
- Lysine
- Methionine + cystine
- Phenylalanine + tyrosine
- Threonine
- Tryptophan
- Valine
- Chloride

It is best to avoid giving your dog human foods with a lot of sodium and preservatives. Water is also absolutely essential to keep your dog healthy. Make a habit of checking your dog's water bowl several times a day so that your dog does not get dehydrated.

Proteins and Amino Acids

Since dogs are carnivores, protein is one of the most important nutrients in a healthy dog's diet. (Dogs should not eat as much meat as their close wolf relatives do. Dogs' diets and needs have changed significantly since they have become human companions.) Proteins contain the necessary amino acids for your dog to produce glucose, which is essential for giving your dog energy. A lack of protein in your dog's diet will result in him being lethargic. His coat may start to look dull, and he is likely to lose weight. Conversely, if your dog gets too much protein, his body will store the excess protein as fat, and he will gain weight.

Meat is the best source of protein for your dog, and a dog's dietary needs are significantly different from a human's needs. If you plan to feed your dog a vegetarian diet, it is very important that you talk to your vet first. It is incredibly difficult to ensure that a carnivore receives adequate protein while on a vegetarian diet. Puppies, in particular, need to have adequate protein to be healthy adults, so you may need to give your puppy a diet with meat, then switch to a vegetarian diet after your Weimaraner becomes an adult.

Protein is particularly important for taking care of your Weimaraner's coat. While you don't want to be excessive, do make sure that your dog gets adequate protein every day. This will be easier if you make meals for your dog. If you don't have time, make sure to buy foods that are high in protein.

Fat and Fatty Acids

Most fats that your dog needs are found in meat. Seed oils provide a lot of the necessary healthy fats, too, with peanut butter being one of the most common sources. Fats break down into fatty acids, which your dog needs for fat-soluble vitamins that help with regular cell functions.

Chapter 14: Nutrition

Perhaps the most obvious benefit of fats and fatty acids can be seen in your dog's coat. Your Weimaraner's coat will look and feel much healthier when he is getting the right nutrients.

The following is a list of potential health issues that might arise if your dog does not get adequate fats in his daily diet:

- His coat will look less healthy.
- His skin may be dry and itchy.
- His immune system could be compromised, making it easier for your dog to get sick.
- He may have an increased risk of heart disease. The primary concern if your dog gets too much fat is that he will become obese, leading to additional health problems.

Photo Courtesy of Kimberly Marx

Carbohydrates and Cooked Foods

Dogs have been living with humans for millennia, so their dietary needs have evolved like our own. They can eat foods with carbohydrates to supplement the energy typically provided by proteins and fats. If you cook grains (such as barley, corn, and rice) prior to feeding them to your dog, it will be easier for him to digest those complex carbohydrates. Note that if your dog is allergic to grains, potatoes and sweet potatoes are also high in carbohydrates.

Different Dietary Requirements for Different Life Stages

Different stages of a dog's life have different nutritional needs. One breeder provided some insight into what you can likely expect when you bring your puppy home, then how things will change over the years.

> *Your breeder has likely sent you home with a weeks worth of food, transition to any new food slowly over a week and pay attention to their stools, should be firm, not loose and easily passed. Use a good quality dog food, made with human grade ingredients that is made and sourced in the United States. You won't find this in a grocery store. Try to rotate a quality food every 5-6 months so they are not being fed the same ingredients and nutrients constantly. A Weimaraner should have interest in their food and readily eat when fed, twice a day is best for digestion, minimizing gulping of food if they're really hungry. This will minimize excess air in the stomach which can contribute to bloat, a life threatening emergency requiring emergency surgery. It also allows you to pick up on any problems sooner.*
>
> **KYRA SCHLIEMAN**
> *SilverLining Weimaraners*

Puppy Food

During the first 12 months of their lives, puppies' bodies are growing. Their nutritional needs are much different from their adult counterparts. To be healthy, they need more calories and have different nutritional needs to promote growth, so feed them a food made specifically for puppies. Puppies can have up to four meals a day. Just be careful not to overfeed them, particularly if you use treats during training.

Adult Dog Food

The primary difference between puppy food and adult dog food is puppy food is higher in calories and nutrients. Dog food manufacturers reduce these nutrients in adult dog food, as adults no longer need lots of calories to sustain growth. As a rule, when a canine reaches about 90% of his predicted adult size, you should switch to adult dog food.

The size of your Weimaraner and the level of activity is key in determining how much to feed him. The following table is a general recommendation for your adult Weimaraner's daily food consumption. Initially, you may want to focus on the calories as you try to find the right balance for your dog.

Dog Size	Calories per day
70 – 100 lbs.	1,680 during hot months 2,500 during cold months
100 + lbs.	2,400 during hot months 3,600 during cold months

To minimize the risk of bloat (covered in Chapter 17), you should feed your Weimaraner at least twice a day (rather than feeding him just one big meal), so you can divide up the calories according to this schedule. Keep in mind these recommendations are per day and not per meal. To make sure your dog feels like a real part of the family, let your pup eat when you do, even if he doesn't get that much food at a time.

It is also recommended that you set the food and water bowls at an elevated level so that your dog doesn't have to lean over so far to eat. This can help reduce the risk of bloat as well. If you notice your Weimaraner eating too quickly, consider a dog feeder that limits how quickly he can eat. After 15 minutes, pick up the food bowl so that he does not continuously eat over the course of the day. However, always leave fresh water out for your dog, making it easily accessible all day and night.

If you plan to add wet food to your dog's diet, pay attention to the total calorie intake and adjust how much you feed your dog between the kibble and wet food. The total calories in the kibble and wet food should balance out so as not to exceed your dog's needs. The same is true if you give your dog a lot of treats over the course of the day. You should factor treat calories into how much you feed your dog at mealtimes.

If you feed your dog homemade food (discussed later in this chapter), you should learn your nutrition facts, and you should pay close attention to calories instead of cup measurements.

Senior Dog Food

> *Change to a senior diet when your dog starts slowing down.*
>
> **CHRISTINE GRISELL**
> *Nani's Weimaraners*

Senior dogs are not always capable of being as active as they were in their younger days. If you notice your dog is slowing down or suffers joint pain and shows a lack of stamina when taking long walks, you can assume your Weimaraner is entering his senior years. Consult with your vet if you think it is time to change the type of food you feed your dog.

The primary difference between adult and senior dog food is senior dog food contains less fat and more antioxidants to help fight weight gain. Senior dogs also need more protein, which will probably make your dog happy because that usually means more meat. Protein helps to maintain your dog's aging muscles. He should also be eating less phosphorus during his golden years to avoid the risk of developing hyperphosphatemia. This is a condition where dogs have excessive amounts of phosphorus in their bloodstream, and older dogs are at greater risk of developing it. The level of phosphorus in the body is controlled by the kidneys; as such, elevated levels of phosphorus are usually an indication of a problem with the kidneys.

Senior dog food has the correct number of calories for reduced activity, which means no adjustment of quantity is needed unless you notice weight gain. Consult your vet if you notice your dog is putting on weight because this could be a sign of illness.

Your Dog's Meal Options

> *Keep it simple with just a high-quality kibble. No human food as treats, ever. If you decide to feed raw or home-cooked meals, you better do your studying, as it's not easy to continually and consistently provide complete and adequate dog dietary needs home-cooked style. What happens if you have an emergency or need to be gone for an extended time and nobody else knows how to feed or cook for the dog on its high-maintenance diet ?... Best to keep it simple and clean, feed high-quality kibble, and no other stuff on the side.*
>
> JESSICA HANSON
> *Hanson Weimaraners*

You have three primary choices for what to feed your dog, or you can use a combination of the three, depending on your situation and your dog's specific needs.

Commercial Food

Make sure that you are buying the best dog food you can afford. Take the time to research each of your options, particularly the nutritional value of the food, and review this annually. Make sure the food you are giving your dog is high quality, and always take into account your dog's size, energy level, and age. Your puppy may not need puppy food for as long as other breeds, and dog food for seniors may not be necessary for

Photo Courtesy of Eric Gray

Weimaraners. You'll need to pay attention to your dog's individual needs to determine if he needs a special food for his age.

The website Pawster provides several great articles about which commercial dog foods are best for Weimaraners. Since new foods frequently come on the market, check periodically to see if there are new, better foods that have become available.

Chapter 14: Nutrition

If you aren't sure which brand of food is best, talk with the breeder about the foods they recommend. Breeders are really the best guides for you, as they are experts. But you can also ask your vet.

Some dogs may be picky eaters that get tired of repeatedly eating the same food. While you shouldn't frequently change the brand of food because that can upset your dog's stomach, you can get foods that have assorted flavors. You can also change the taste by adding a bit of wet (canned) food. Adding one-fourth to one-third of a can for each meal is an easy change to make to ensure your dog's happiness.

For more details on commercial options, check out the website *Dog Food Advisor*. They provide reviews on various dog food brands, as well as information on recalls and contamination issues.

Commercial Dry Food

Dry dog food is what the vast majority of people feed their dogs.

Dry Dog Food

PROS	CONS
• Convenience	• Requires research to ensure you don't buy doggy junk food
• Variety	• Packaging is not always honest
• Availability	• Recalls for food contamination
• Affordability	• Loose FDA nutritional regulations
• Manufacturers follow nutritional recommendations. (Not all of them follow this, so do your brand research before you buy.)	• Low-quality food may have questionable ingredients
• Specially formulated for different canine life-stages	
• Can be used for training	
• Easy to store	

The convenience and ease on your budget mean you are almost certainly going to buy kibble for your dog. This is perfectly fine, and most dogs will be more than happy to eat kibble. Be sure you know what brand

you are feeding your dog, and pay attention to kibble recalls so you can stop feeding your dog a certain brand if necessary. Check out the following sites regularly for recall information:
- Dog Food Recalls – www.dogfoodadvisor.com
- American Kennel Club – www.AKC.org
- Dog Food Guide – www.dogfood.guide

Commercial Wet Food

Most dogs prefer wet dog food over kibble, but it is also more expensive. Wet dog food can be purchased in large packs that can be extremely easy to store.

Wet Dog Food

PROS	CONS
• Helps keep dogs hydrated	• Dog bowls must be washed after every meal
• Has a richer scent and flavor	• Can soften bowel movements
• Easier to eat for dogs with dental problems (particularly those with missing teeth) or if a dog has been ill	• Can be messier than kibble
	• Once opened, it has a short shelf-life and should be covered and refrigerated
• Convenient and easy to serve	• More expensive than dry dog food and comes in small quantities
• Unopened, it can last between one and three years	• Packaging is not always honest
• Balanced based on current pet nutrition recommendations	• Recalls for food contamination
	• Loose FDA regulations

Like dry dog food, wet dog food is convenient, and picky dogs are much more likely to eat it than kibble. If your dog gets sick, use wet dog food to ensure that he is still eating and gets the necessary nutrition each day. It may be harder to switch back to kibble once your Weimaraner is healthy, but you can always add a little wet food to make each meal more appetizing.

Raw Diet

For dogs prone to food allergies, raw diets can help prevent an allergic reaction to wheat and processed foods. Raw diets are heavy in raw meats, bones, vegetables, and specific supplements. Some of the benefits of a raw diet include the following:
- Improves your dog's coat and skin
- Improves immune system
- Improves health (as a result of better digestion)
- Increases energy
- Increases muscle mass

Raw diets are meant to give your dog the kind of food canines ate before they became domesticated. It means giving your dog uncooked meats, whole (uncooked) bones, and a small amount of dairy products. It doesn't include processed food of any kind—not even food cooked in your kitchen.

There are potential risks to this diet. Dogs have been domesticated for millennia, and their digestive systems have also evolved. Trying to force them to eat the kind of diet they ate hundreds of years ago does not always work as intended, primarily because dogs' digestive systems have evolved, so they process raw meat differently than they once did.

There are also many risks associated with feeding dogs uncooked meals, particularly if the food has been contaminated. Things like bacteria pose a serious risk and can be transferred to you if your dog gets sick. Many medical professionals also warn about the dangers of giving dogs bones, even if they are uncooked. Bones can splinter in your dog's mouth and puncture the esophagus or stomach.

The *Canine Journal* (www.caninejournal.com) provides a lot of information about a raw diet, including different recipes and how to transition your dog to this diet. Always talk to your veterinarian before putting your dog on a new kind of diet.

Homemade Diet

The best home-cooked meals should be planned in advance so that your Weimaraner gets the correct nutritional balance. Typically, 50% of your dog's food should be animal protein (fish, poultry, and organ meats). About 25% should be full of complex carbohydrates. The remaining 25% should be from fruits and vegetables, particularly foods like pumpkin, apples, bananas, and green beans. These foods provide extra flavor your Weimaraner will probably love while filling him up faster and reducing the chance of overeating.

The following are a few sites where you can learn how to make homemade meals for canines. They are not breed-specific, so if you have more than one dog, these meals can be made for all your furry canine friends:

- Hublore (http://hublore.blogspot.com/2011/05/homemade-dog-food-recipe.html)
- Homemade Dog Food with a Special Ingredient (https://pethelpful.com/dogs/Homemade-Dog-Food-with-an-Extra-Special-Ingredient)
- Canine Journal (https://www.caninejournal.com/homemade-dog-food-recipes/)
- DIY Homemade Dog Food (https://damndelicious.net/2015/04/27/diy-homemade-dog-food/)

Keep in mind the foods your Weimaraner absolutely should not eat. You can also mix some of the food you make for yourself into your Weimaraner's meal. Do not feed your Weimaraner from your plate! Split the food, placing your dog's meal into a bowl so that your canine understands your food is just for you.

Scheduling Meals

Your Weimaraner will probably expect you to stick to a schedule, which definitely includes mealtimes. If treats and snacks are something you establish as a normal routine, your dog will expect that too!

For puppies, plan to have three or four meals, while adults and seniors should typically have two meals a day.

Food Allergies and Intolerance

Whenever you start your dog on a new type of food (even if it's simply a different flavor), you need to monitor him while he becomes accustomed to the change. Food allergies are fairly common in Weimaraners, and the symptoms manifest themselves as hot spots, which are similar to rashes in humans. Your dog may start scratching or chewing specific spots on his body, and his fur or hair could start falling out around those spots. Some dogs don't have individual hot spots, but the allergy shows up on their entire coat. If your Weimaraner seems to be shedding more hair than normal, take him to the vet to be checked for food allergies.

If you give your dog something his stomach cannot handle, it will probably be obvious when your dog is unable to hold his bowels. If he is already house-trained, he will probably either pant at you or whimper to let you know he needs to go outside. Get him outside as quickly as you can so that he does not have an accident. Flatulence will also probably occur more often if your Weimaraner has a food intolerance.

Since the symptoms of food allergies and intolerances look similar to a reaction to nutritional deficiencies, you should visit your vet immediately! This is especially true if you notice any problems with your dog's coat or skin.

CHAPTER 15

Grooming – Productive Bonding

When it comes to grooming, it doesn't get much easier than the Weimaraner, at least when it comes to how much cleaning they need. The more time you spend outside with your dog, the more grooming you'll need to do – such as looking for parasites and cleaning up mud. On a daily basis though, this is a dog that is going to be easy to groom. As one breeder pointed out about Weimaraners:

Chapter 15: Grooming – Productive Bonding

> *They are mostly wash and wear dogs. A nice bath occasionally, taking care to clean out ears.*
>
> ANNE TYSON
> *Regen Weimaraners*

Weimaraners can be a dream when it comes to maintenance as long as you train them well. If you don't train your Weimaraner, you are in for a fight when bathing him and clipping his nails. Otherwise, they have short hair, so even though they do shed, it's not going to accumulate as it does with a lot of other breeds. Shedding is easy to manage with a Weimaraner.

Then there are the other regular grooming tasks, such as brushing your dog's teeth and trimming his nails. If you find that you simply can't get your Weimaraner to sit still for a nail clipping, or if your Weimaraner has a blood disorder (covered in Chapter 17), it is best to pay a professional to take care of those nails.

Grooming Focus and Tools

Most Weimaraner grooming needs can be done at home. There are still a few things that we strongly recommend seeing an expert about in the early days to learn how to take care of your Weimaraner (all paw related), but for the most part, you should be able to take care of your dog yourself. You'll also appreciate the help since your Weimaraner is probably going to be incredibly rambunctious and difficult to calm down for paw care. With proper training, your Weimaraner can learn to endure grooming, actually realizing that it is dedicated time with you! It is also healthier for the dog if you do most of the grooming, as there are some issues that you are more likely to notice if you brush him daily (see Chapters 16 and 17). Between your Weimaraner very likely having allergies and this being a breed that is prone to skin tumors, regular coat care can help you catch issues before they become serious.

Here's a quick summary of the best tools to take care of your Weimaraner's coat:
- Rubber brush—and you can get a grooming glove to make it feel more like extra petting time instead of work
- Shampoo (Make sure you use dog shampoo, not human, and check Bark Space for the latest recommendations.)
- Nail trimmers and boar bristle brush
- Toothbrush and dog toothpaste (not human—it's toxic for dogs!) (Check the AKC for the latest recommendations for the Weimaraner, as they tend to have dental problems.)

Coat Management

> *Grooming the Weimaraner is easy and is one of the things many owners find appealing about the breed. Yes, they do shed short gray hairs, but it is minimal compared to many other breeds, especially if the dog is kept brushed and bathed. A rubber brush to the coat every two to three days will keep shedding to a minimum, keep the coat shiny, improve circulation, and alert you to any problem lumps early if you're paying attention. It helps create a bonding time with your dog and, if done correctly, most Weimaraners enjoy it; after all, they're monopolizing their time with you, one of their favorite pastimes.*
>
> KYRA SCHLIEMAN
> *SilverLining Weimaraners*

Weimaraners do shed, so to reduce the amount of dog hair around your home, it is best to brush your dog daily. They have sensitive skin, so don't apply too much pressure when brushing.

Always make sure to tire your dog before you start brushing. You'll know when you don't need to dedicate time to tiring your dog when he starts to slow down as a senior or shows an interest in just sitting and letting you pet and brush him.

Puppies

The difficulty when grooming a puppy is fairly universal because puppies are notorious for squirming! A daily brushing is the best way to bond with your dog and get him accustomed to grooming. Yes, it will be a bit challenging in the beginning because puppies don't sit still for prolonged periods of time; there will be a lot of wiggling and attempts to play. Trying to tell your puppy that the brush is not a toy clearly won't work, so be patient during each brushing session!

On the other hand, your pup will be so adorable that you probably won't mind a grooming session taking a bit longer than expected. Just make sure you let your pup know grooming is serious business, and playing comes after grooming. Otherwise, your Weimaraner is going to always try to play, which will make brushing time-consuming.

Try planning to brush your puppy after a vigorous exercise session. If you find your puppy has trouble sitting still, you can make brushing sessions shorter, but do it more than once a day until he gets used to the routine.

Adult Dogs

Brushing needs to be done at least once a week for the adults, especially after a lot of outdoor activity. The grooming process stimulates the skin to release oils that make the fur shinier and more resistant to dirt. This is absolutely necessary for Weimaraners. If you regularly brush your dog, it can help reduce how often you have to bathe him.

Brushing your dog is about more than just removing excess fur and improving the coat's shine. You need to spend each grooming session looking for skin problems, lumps, flea or tick bites, and other problems

> **HELPFUL TIP**
>
> **How Much Do They Shed?**
>
> Weimaraners are moderate shedders and tend to shed more of their short gray hair in autumn and spring. A grooming glove is an excellent tool for Weimaraner owners and can help remove loose fur before it ends up on your floors and furniture. Grooming gloves are usually made from rubber or soft plastic, and in addition to removing loose fur, they can help distribute natural oils to keep your Weimaraner's coat looking its best.

when you brush your buddy. This will reveal any potential issues that you should monitor and follow up with a trip to the vet if symptoms become severe.

If you rescued an adult Weimaraner, it might take a little while to get the dog used to being brushed frequently. If your dog does not feel comfortable in the beginning when you brush his fur, work the routine into your schedule, just like training, so he will get accustomed to the task.

Senior Dogs

You can brush your senior dog more often if you would like, as the extra affection and time you give him will likely be welcome. The grooming process can be incredibly welcome in older Weimaraners. After all, he's slowing down, and just relaxing with you will be enjoyable for him (and the warmth of your hands will feel really good on his aging body). Grooming sessions are an appropriate time to check for problems while giving your older pup a nice massage to ease any pain. Look for any changes to the skin, such as bumps or fatty lumps. These may need to be mentioned to the vet during a regular visit.

Allergies

Many Weimaraners have skin allergies, so keep an eye out for hot spots, or if you notice your dog's coat is thinning, then you should look for the following allergic reactions:
- Wounds take longer to heal

- Weak immune system
- Aching joints
- Hair is falling out
- Ear infections
- Frequent scratching of the eyes

Regular brushing keeps you aware of the health of your Weimaraner's coat. This will help you identify when your big dear is suffering from allergies so that you can take him to the vet immediately.

In those early days, grooming may seem difficult, so to help you through the process and give you some incentive on keeping it up, here's what one breeder said about grooming your Weimaraner and how it will benefit you a lot down the line.

Bath Time

> *Weimaraners are very low maintenance when it comes to grooming... Try not to bathe them excessively as it could dry out their skin.*
>
> **JOE WIDOMSKI**
> *Shade of Grey Weimaraners*

Baths are recommended roughly every six to eight weeks. If your Weimaraner gets muddy or really dirty, make sure to bathe him so that the dirt and mud don't get trapped in the fur and create worse problems. If you have medicinal shampoo, you will need to wash your dog twice, once with a hypo-allergenic sham poo, and a second time with the medicinal shampoo. Don't' combine them. There's definitely a fine balance to bathing Weimaraners because they require bathing more often than a lot of other dogs, but it is also very easy to over-bathe them, thinking that it will help keep them clean (when it will actually reduce their natural oils).

Make sure the water isn't too cold or too hot but comfortably warm, and always avoid getting your dog's head wet. How to wash your dog's face is covered in the next section.

1. Gather everything you will need before you start your dog's bath. At a minimum, you need the following:
   A. shampoo and conditioners made specifically for dogs
   B. cup for pouring water (if bathing in a tub)
   C. towels
   D. brushes for after the drying process
   E. nonslip tub mat if you use a tub, and
   F. buckets and a hose to rinse off if you bathe your dog outside.
2. Take your Weimaraner out for a walk. This will tire your dog and make him a little hotter and less fearful—he might even appreciate the bath's cooling effect.
3. Run the water, making sure the temperature is lukewarm and not hot, especially if you have just finished a walk. If you are washing your Weimaraner in a bathtub, you only need enough water to cover your pup's stomach. Do not fully cover your dog's body.
4. Pick up your dog if you are using a bathtub, and talk to him in a strong, confident voice.
5. Place the dog in the tub and use the cup to wash the dog. Don't use too much soap—it isn't necessary. You can fully soak the dog, starting at the neck and going to the rump. It is fine to get him wet and suds him up all at once, or you can do it a little at a time if your dog is very wiggly. Just make sure you don't get any water on his head.
6. Confidently talk to your Weimaraner while you are bathing him.
7. Make sure you don't pour water on your dog's head or in his eyes or ears. Use a wet hand and gently scrub. (Follow the steps in the next section for how to carefully wash your dog's face and ears.)
8. When you rinse, make sure to brush up against the fur so that there is no shampoo left.
9. Take your Weimaraner out of the water and towel him dry.

Chapter 15: Grooming – Productive Bonding

10. Make sure to give special attention to drying around the head, face, and wrinkles.
11. Brush your dog when you are finished.
12. Give him a treat if he was particularly upset about the bath.

You can use these practices with other kinds of bathing, such as outside or at a public washing facility; modify the steps as necessary.

The first few times you bathe your dog, pay attention to the things that bother or scare your Weimaraner. If he is afraid of running water, make sure you don't have the water running when your dog is in the tub. If he moves around a lot when you start to apply the shampoo, it could indicate the smell is too strong. Modify the process as necessary in order to make it as comfortable for your dog as possible.

Keep a calm, loving tone as you wash your dog to make the process a little easier next time. Sure, your Weimaraner may whine, throw a tantrum, or wiggle excessively, but a calm reaction will teach your dog that bathing is a necessary part of being a member of the pack.

Cleaning Eyes and Ears

When bathing your dog, use a washcloth to wash his face and ears, and ALWAYS avoid getting water in his ears, which can lead to problems.

You will need to make weekly checks around your Weimaraner's eyes and ears to detect infections early. The following are signs of a problem:
- Frequent head shaking or tilting
- Regular scratching at ears
- Swollen or red ears
- A smell or discharge from the ears

If you notice any problems with your Weimaraner's ears, make an appointment with your vet. Never try to treat an infection on your own; hydrogen peroxide, cotton swabs, and other cleaning tools should never be used in a dog's ears. Your vet can show you how to clean your dog's ears correctly.

Weimaraners have a few genetic eye and ear conditions (See Chapter 17), so always take time to check your dog's eyes while you are grooming him.

Cataracts are a fairly common problem for all dogs as they age. If you see cloudy eyes, have your Weimaraner checked by your vet.

Trimming Nails

If you have never cut a dog's nails before, do NOT start with a Weimaraner. Schedule an appointment with a professional groomer who has worked with large dogs before. There is a lot more work to do than just trimming the nails, and NO novice should ever attempt this grooming activity without a lot of guidance and help. A professional can show you what needs to be done to trim the nails. It is far harder to do with large dogs than with small dogs.

Your professional can tell you what you need to know and let you know how often your dog needs his nails trimmed based on how quickly you help wear down the nails. If you and your Weimaraner spend a lot of time walking on sidewalks and concrete, it will slow the nail growth compared to regular jaunts in woods and dirt paths.

This can seem like a lot, so one breeder provided a wealth of helpful tips for general care of a Weimaraner, especially how to get them more comfortable with brushes and nail trimmings.

> *Get in the habit of weekly nail trimming with a Dremmel grinder or safety nail clipper very early on. Handle the toes and feet frequently without doing trimming, associate it with something pleasant, lots of praise always, treats and fun. It will prevent battles down the road and poor feet in the Weimaraner which is painful when they get that needed exercise!*
>
> KYRA SCHLIEMAN
> *SilverLining Weimaraners*

Oral Health

Weimaraners are prone to dental issues, and that means that you should never skip brushing your dog's teeth. Besides healthy food, there are two recommendations for taking care of your Weimaraner's teeth.
1. Brush your Weimaraner's teeth at least twice a week.
2. Give your Weimaraner dental chew treats.

Brushing Your Dog's Teeth

You have to learn to be patient and keep teeth cleaning from being an all-out fight with your dog. Brushing a dog's teeth is a little weird, and your Weimaraner may not be terribly happy with someone putting stuff in his mouth. However, once he is accustomed to it, the task will likely only take a few minutes a day. Regular brushing keeps down plaque and tartar, making your pup's teeth healthier.

This can be tricky, but it's worth it. As one breeder said about overall grooming:

> *Weimaraners are very low maintenance when it comes to grooming. Main grooming concern would be to keep toenails trimmed and ears cleaned. Get them used to having their teeth brushed which will help as they get older.*
>
> JOE WIDOMSKI
> *Shade of Grey Weimaraner*

Always use a toothpaste that is made for dogs; human toothpaste can be toxic for your big friend. There are assorted flavors of dog toothpaste, which will make it easier when brushing your Weimaraner's teeth, and it could also be entertaining as he tries to eat the meat-flavored toothpaste!

The following are the steps for brushing your dog's teeth:
1. Put a little toothpaste on your finger and hold it out to your dog.
2. Let your dog lick the toothpaste from your finger.
3. Praise your dog for trying something new.
4. Put a little toothpaste on your finger again, lift your dog's upper lip, and begin to rub in circles along your Weimaraner's gums. Your pup will likely make it difficult by constantly trying to lick your finger. Give your puppy praise when he doesn't lick the toothpaste or doesn't wiggle too much.

5. Try to move your finger in a circular motion. This will be very tricky, especially if you have a puppy with sharp baby teeth.
6. Try to keep the dog still without putting him in a vise. As your puppy gets bigger, he'll need to know how to sit for the cleaning process voluntarily.
7. Try to massage both the top and bottom gums. It is likely the first few times you won't be able to do much more than get your finger in your dog's mouth, and that's okay. Over time, your dog will learn to listen because general behavioral training will reinforce listening to your commands.
8. Stay positive. No, you probably won't be able to clean your dog's teeth properly for a while, and that is perfectly fine—as long as you keep working at it patiently and consistently.

Once your dog seems comfortable with having his teeth brushed with your finger, try the same steps with a canine toothbrush. (It could take a couple of weeks before you can graduate to this stage.)

Dental Chews

One of the healthiest treats to give any dog is dental chews. While you will need to keep count of the treats as a part of your dog's daily caloric intake, they help with taking care of your dog's teeth. They aren't a replacement for regular brushing, but they are a good complement. Dogs tend to love these treats, and they help improve your dog's breath, so it is a win-win. Make sure to do your research to ensure that you are giving your dog the healthiest dental chews. You don't want to give your Weimaraner any treats that have questionable or uncertain ingredients.

CHAPTER 16

General Health Issues: Allergies, Parasites, and Vaccinations

As a breed that loves the outdoors, allergies and parasites are going to be concerns for your dog. It will be well worth it to enjoy all of those outdoor activities, especially with as enthusiastic as your dog will be. It just means that you will need to be more vigilant with your dog's health than if you had a more sedentary, home-body canine.

Odds are pretty good that your Weimaraner will have allergies because allergies are very common for this breed. For the most part, Weimaraner allergies appear on the skin, with rashes and hair loss being quite common, but sometimes they may scratch at their eyes. Adopting a daily brushing schedule will ensure that you not only notice rashes but will also be able to find any potential parasites infecting the exterior of your dog. If you notice your Weimaraner pawing at his eyes, this could also be a sign of allergies.

Environmental factors largely determine whether or not your dog gets parasites. For example, if you live near a wooded area, your dog is at a greater risk of having ticks than a dog that lives in the city. Fleas are a universal problem for all dogs because fleas can live in any grass, short or long. If you notice rashes or signs of skin irritation, it could be an allergic reaction or symptoms of a parasite. Talk to your vet about potential environmental risks and any skin conditions you notice when you groom your dog.

Chapter 16: General Health Issues: Allergies, Parasites, and Vaccinations

The Role of Your Veterinarian

> *Annual vet care is vitally important as the Weimaraner ages. A good vet will thoroughly examine the dog, watching or investigating the inevitable lumps and bumps that will often appear on the Weimaraner's sleek body. They should do a yearly routine blood panel, which can detect specific problems that are more easily treated or cured if caught early.*
>
> KYRA SCHLIEMAN
> *SilverLining Weimaraners*

Scheduled veterinary visits, routine vaccinations, and regular check-ups make for a healthy Weimaraner. If your dog seems sluggish or less excited than usual, it could be a sign there is something wrong with him. Fortunately, the breed's personality tends to make it easy to tell when your dog isn't feeling well. Annual visits to the vet will help catch any problems that might be slowly draining the energy or the health from your dog.

Regular check-ups also ensure that your Weimaraner is aging well. If your dog shows symptoms of a potential problem, an early diagnosis will address the problem. You and your vet can create a plan to manage any pain or problems that come with your dog's aging process. The vet may recommend adjustments to your schedule to accommodate your pup's aging body and

HEALTH ALERT!
Von Willebrand's Disease (vWD)

Von Willebrand's Disease (vWD) is a genetic blood clotting disorder common in humans and dogs. Wei-maraners may be slightly more prone to developing this disease than some other breeds. Symptoms of vWD are tricky to spot and may only present as a spontaneous hemorrhage or uncontrolled bleeding after surgery. However, your veterinarian can perform a screening test called buccal mucosal screening to iden-tify this disease before surgery or other procedures.

diminishing abilities. This will ensure that the two of you can keep having fun together without hurting your dog.

Vets can provide treatment or preventive medication for parasites and other microscopic threats that your dog might encounter on a daily basis, whether playing outside or when he is exposed to dogs or other animals.

Allergies

Allergies are a common problem for Weimaraners; if you see your dog scratching a lot, there are very good odds the problem is allergies. Dog allergies are usually a result of allergens (such as dust, mold, or pollen), which irritate the skin or nasal passages. Dogs often develop allergies when they are between one and five years old. Once they develop an allergy, canines never outgrow the problem.

The scientific name for environmental allergies is atopic dermatitis. However, it is difficult to know if the problem is environmental or if it is a food you are feeding your dog.

The following symptoms can be seen when either type of allergy is present:
- Itching/scratching, particularly around the face
- Hot spots
- Ear infections
- Skin infections
- Runny eyes and nose (not as common)

Since the symptoms are the same for food and environmental allergies, your vet will help determine the cause. If your dog has a food allergy, change the food that you give him. If he has an environmental allergy, he will need medication, just as humans do. There are several types of medications that can help your dog become less sensitive to allergens:
- Antibacterial/Antifungal – These treatments only address the problems that come with allergies; shampoos, pills, and creams usually do not directly treat the allergy itself.

- Anti-inflammatories – These are over-the-counter medications that are comparable to allergy medicine for people. Don't give your dog any medication without first consulting with the vet. You will need to monitor your dog to see if he has any adverse effects. If your dog is lethargic, has diarrhea, or shows signs of dehydration, consult with your vet immediately.
- Immunotherapy – This is a series of shots that can help reduce your dog's sensitivity to whatever he is allergic to. You can learn from your vet how to give your dog these shots at home. Scientists are also developing an oral version of this medication to make it easier to take care of your dog.
- Topical – This medication is usually a type of shampoo and conditioner that will remove any allergens from your dog's fur. Giving your dog a warm (not hot) bath can also help relieve itching.

To determine the best treatment for your situation, talk with your vet.

Inhalant and Environmental Allergies

Inhalant allergies are caused by things like dust, pollen, mold, and dog dander. Your dog might scratch at a particular hot spot, or he might paw at his eyes and ears. Some dogs have runny noses and sneeze prolifically, in addition to scratching.

Contact Allergies

Contact allergies mean that your dog has touched something that triggers an allergic reaction. Substances like wool, chemicals in a flea treatment, and certain grasses can trigger irritation in a dog's skin, even causing discoloration. If left untreated, the allergic reaction can cause the affected area to emit a strong odor or cause fur loss.

Like food allergies, contact allergies are easy to treat because once you know what is irritating your dog's skin, you can remove the problem.

Fleas and Ticks

Make it a habit to check for ticks after every outing into the woods or near long grass or wild plants. Comb through your dog's fur and check his skin for signs of irritation and for any parasites. Since you will be brushing him several times a week, you should be able to recognize when there's a change, such as a new bump.

Fleas are problematic because they're far more mobile than ticks. The best way to look for fleas is to make it a regular part of your brushing sessions. If you see black specks on the comb after brushing through your dog's fur, this could be a sign of fleas.

Instead of using a comb, you can also put your dog on a white towel and run your hand over his fur. Fleas and flea dirt are likely to fall onto the towel. Fleas often are seen on the stomach, so you may notice them when your pup wants a belly rub. You can also look for behavioral indicators, such as incessant scratching and licking. If fleas are a problem, you will need to use flea-preventative products on a regular basis once your puppy has reached the appropriate age.

Both fleas and ticks can carry parasites and illnesses that can be passed on to you and your family. Ticks carry Lyme disease, which can be debilitating or deadly if untreated. Lyme disease symptoms include headaches, fever, and fatigue. The bite itself often has a red circle around it.

Ticks will fall off your dog once they are full, so if you find a tick on your dog, it will either be looking for a place to latch onto your dog, or it will be feeding. Use the following steps to remove the tick if it has latched onto your dog.

1. Apply rubbing alcohol to the area where the tick is located.

Photo Courtesy of Annabella Alfaro

2. Use tweezers to pull the tick off your dog. Do not use your fingers because infections are transmitted through blood, and you don't want the tick to latch onto you.
3. Place the tick in a bag and make sure it is secure so that it does not fall out. The vet can assess the type of tick for diagnostic purposes since different types of ticks carry different diseases.
4. Examine the spot where the tick was to make sure it is fully removed. Sometimes the head will remain under the dog's skin, so make sure all of the tick has been removed.
5. Set up a meeting with the vet to have your dog checked.

The FDA has issued a warning about some store-bought treatments for fleas and ticks. Treatments can be applied monthly, or you can purchase a collar for constant protection. Either way, make sure the treatment does not contain isoxazoline, which can have a negative effect on some pets. (This chemical is found in Bravecto, Nexgard, Credelio, and Simparica.)

Most ingredients in these treatments are safe if the proper dose is used. However, if you use a product that is meant for a larger dog, the effects can be toxic to your smaller dog or not as effective if you use a dosage meant for a smaller dog on your large dog. Consult your vet for recommended treatments and administer the appropriate dose of flea and tick repellant for your dog's size and needs. When you start applying the treatment, watch your dog for the following issues:
- Diarrhea/vomiting
- Trembling
- Lethargy
- Seizures

Take your dog to the vet if you notice any of these issues.

Never use any cat product on a dog and vice versa. If your dog is sick, pregnant, or nursing, you may need to look for an alternative preventative treatment. If you have a cat or young children, you should choose one of the other preventative options for keeping fleas and ticks away. This is because flea collars contain an ingredient that is lethal to felines and which might be carcinogenic to humans.

The packaging on flea treatments will advise you when to begin treating your dog based on his current age and size. Different brands have different recommendations, and you don't want to start treating your puppy too early. There are also important steps to applying the treatment. Make sure you understand all of the steps before purchasing the flea treatment.

If you want to use natural products instead of chemicals, research the alternatives and decide what works best for your Weimaraner. Verify that any natural products work before you buy them, and make sure you consult with your vet. Establish a regular monthly schedule and add it to your calendar so that you remember to consistently treat your dog for fleas and ticks.

Parasitic Worms

Although worms are a less common problem in dogs than fleas and ticks, they can be far more dangerous. The following lists the types of worms that you should be aware of:

- Heartworms
- Hookworms
- Roundworms
- Tapeworms
- Whipworms

Unfortunately, there isn't an easy-to-recognize set of symptoms to help identify when your dog has worms. However, you can keep an eye out for the following symptoms, and if your dog shows any of these warning signs, schedule a visit to the vet:

- Your Weimaraner is unexpectedly lethargic for a few days.
- Patches of fur begin to fall out (this will be noticeable if you brush your Weimaraner regularly), or you notice patchy spaces in your dog's coat.
- Your dog's stomach becomes distended (expands) and looks like a potbelly.

- Your Weimaraner begins coughing or vomiting, has diarrhea, or has a loss of appetite.

If you aren't sure about any symptom, it's always best to get your dog to the vet as soon as possible.

Heartworms

Heartworms are a significant threat to your dog's health and can be deadly as they can both slow and stop blood flow. As such, you should consistently treat your dog with heartworm protection.

Fortunately, there are medications that prevent your dog from developing heartworms. To prevent this deadly problem, you can give your dog a chewable medication, use a topical medicine, or request shots.

The heartworm parasite is carried by mosquitoes, and it is a condition that is costly and time-consuming to treat. The following are the steps involved in treating your dog for heartworms:

- The vet will draw blood for testing, which can cost as much as $1,000.
- Treatment will begin with some initial medications, including antibiotics and anti-inflammatory drugs.
- Following a month of the initial medication, your vet will give your dog three shots over the course of two months.

From the time of diagnosis until the confirmation your dog is free of heartworms, you will need to be extremely cautious when you exercise your dog because the worms are in his heart, and that inhibits blood flow. This means raising your dog's heart rate too much could kill him. Your vet will tell you how best to exercise your canine during this time. Considering your Weimaraner may want to be energetic, this could be a very rough time for both you and your dog.

Treatment will continue after the shots are complete. After approximately six months, your vet will conduct another blood test to ensure the worms are gone.

Once your dog is cleared of the parasites, you will need to begin medicating your dog against heartworms in the future. There will be lasting damage to your dog's heart, so you will need to ensure that your dog does not overexercise.

Intestinal Worms: Hookworms, Roundworms, Tapeworms, and Whipworms

All four of these worms thrive in your dog's intestinal tract, and they get there when your dog eats something contaminated. The following are the most common ways dogs ingest worms:
- Feces
- Small hosts, such as fleas, cockroaches, earthworms, and rodents
- Soil, including licking it from their fur and paws
- Contaminated water
- Mother's milk (If the mother dog has worms, she can pass them on to young puppies when they nurse.)

The following are the most common symptoms and problems caused by intestinal parasites:
- Anemia
- Blood loss
- Coughing
- Dehydration
- Diarrhea
- Large intestine inflammation
- Weight loss
- A pot-bellied appearance

If a dog lies in soil with **hookworm larvae**, the parasites can burrow through the canine's skin. Vets will conduct a diagnostic test to determine if your dog has this parasite, and if your dog does have hookworms, the vet will prescribe a dewormer. If your dog is infested with hookworms,

Chapter 16: General Health Issues: Allergies, Parasites, and Vaccinations

you should visit a doctor yourself because humans can get hookworms too. Being treated at the same time as your Weimaraner will help stop the vicious cycle of continually trading off which of you has hookworms.

Photo Courtesy of Missy Doudna

Roundworms are quite common, and at some point in their lives, most dogs have to be treated for them. The parasites primarily eat the digested food in your dog's stomach, getting the nutrients your dog needs. It is possible for larvae to remain in your dog's stomach even after all the adult worms have been eradicated. If your Weimaraner is pregnant, her puppies should be checked periodically to make sure the inactive larvae are not passed on to the puppies. The mother will also need to go through the same testing to make sure the worms don't make her sick.

Tapeworms are usually eaten when they are eggs and are carried by fleas or from the feces of other animals that also have tapeworms. The eggs develop in the canine's small intestine until they reach the adult stage. Over time, parts of the tapeworm will break off and can be seen in your dog's waste. If this happens, you should be very thorough when cleaning up any waste so other animals will not also contract tapeworms. While tapeworms are not usually fatal, they can cause weight loss and give your dog a potbelly. (The size of your dog's stomach depends on how big the worms grow in your dog's intestines.)

Your vet can test your dog for tapeworms and can prescribe medication to take care of the problem. The medication might include chewable tablets, regular tablets, or a powder that can be sprinkled on your dog's food. There is a minimal risk of humans catching tapeworms, but children are at the greatest risk. Be sure children wash their hands carefully when playing in areas used by your dog. It is also possible to contract tapeworms if a person swallows a flea, which is feasible if your dog and home have a serious infestation.

Whipworms grow in the large intestine, and when in large numbers, they can be fatal. Their name is indicative of the appearance of their tails, which are thinner than their upper section. Like the other worms, you will need to have your dog tested to determine if he has acquired whipworms.

Staying current with flea treatments, properly disposing of your pet's waste, and making sure your Weimaraner does not eat trash or animal waste will help prevent your dog from getting these parasites.

Medication to prevent these four parasites can often be included in your dog's heartworm medication. Be sure to speak with your vet regarding the different options.

Vaccinating Your Weimaraner

Vaccination schedules are routine for most dog breeds, including Weimaraners. Make sure to add this information to your calendar, and until your puppy has completed his vaccinations, he should avoid contact with other dogs.

The following list can help you schedule your Weimaraner's vaccinations:

Timeline	Shot		
6 to 8 weeks	Bordetella Lyme	Leptospira Influenza Virus-H3N8	DHPP – First shot Influenza Virus-H3N2
10 to 12 weeks	Leptospira Lyme	DHPP – Second Rabies shot Influenza Virus-H3N8	Influenza Virus-H3N2
14 to 16 weeks	DHPP – Third shot		
Annually	Leptospira Lyme	Bordetella Influenza Virus-H3N8	Rabies Influenza Virus-H3N2
Every 3 years	DHPP Booster	Rabies (if opting for a longer-duration vaccination)	

These shots protect your dog against a range of ailments. Keep in mind these shots should be a part of your dog's annual vet visit so you can continue to keep your pup safe!

Holistic Alternatives

Wanting to prevent exposure to chemical treatments for your dog makes sense, and there are many good reasons why people are moving to more holistic methods. However, if you decide to go with holistic medication, talk with your vet first about reputable options. You can also seek out Weimaraner experts for recommendations before you start trying any holistic methods of care.

It is possible something like massage therapy can help your dog, especially as he ages. Even chiropractic therapy is available for dogs, but you will need to be sure to find a reputable chiropractor for your pup so that the treatment doesn't do more harm than good. Follow recommendations on reputable, holistic Weimaraner websites to provide the best, safest care for your dog.

Photo Courtesy of Jeff Daugherty

CHAPTER 17

Genetic Health Concerns Common to the Weimaraner

Though generally a healthier large dog that is likely to live a longer than average life span, the Weimaraner does have some serious health issues. You will need to monitor for these ailments to make sure your good boy has a long, healthy life. Since some of these diseases can be very expensive to treat, Weimaraners can be more costly to insure.

Proper care, including watching your dog's weight can help keep your dog from having a lot of issues. Chapter 15 covered how to keep your dog healthy with a good diet, and 16 covered how to protect your dog from

Photo Courtesy of April James

outside risks. This chapter focuses on genetic issues, their symptoms, and how the ailments are treated. It also covers the kinds of ailments that come with age, something that you will likely start to notice by the time he is eight years old.

Common Weimaraner Health Issues

You want to make sure that you catch health issues early to improve your dog's quality of life. Take the time to monitor your dog for those potential health problems.

Von Willebrand's Disease

This is a fairly common blood disease for larger breeds and is similar to hemophilia in humans. A dog with this disorder needs adequate amounts of protein to ensure that their blood properly clots. While all dogs need adequate protein in their diet, a dog with Von Willebrand's Disease can bleed excessively when they don't get adequate protein. It is a serious illness, but fortunately it is easy to detect and to treat.

Vets can conduct a blood screening even if your dog isn't presenting any symptoms so you know if your Weimaraner has this disease. If the test comes back positive, you will need to be more attentive to when your dog is injured since he will bleed a lot faster and more than a dog without the issue. It may also be necessary for you to avoid giving your dog some types of medication as it can exacerbate the issue.

Hemophilia A

Another serious blood disease that affects the dog's blood from being able to adequately clot. If a dog has this disorder, cuts have to be immediately treated to stop the bleeding. A special medication has been made to help stem the flow of blood, and it must be applied for any cut to make sure that the dog doesn't lose too much blood. Even small cuts are much more serious for a dog with Hemophilia A.

Most dogs (and people) who have this problem are likely to suffer from mild anemia because such an active dog is likely to get hurt regularly. In the worst cases, it can lead to a dog's death. The disease can be detected in a blood screening, and all vets who treat the dog will need to know that it is a problem for your dog to make sure that all precautions are taken during a dog's treatment.

Hip and Elbow Dysplasia

Hip and elbow dysplasia are common ailments for medium- and larger-sized dogs. Their diet (Chapter 14) as a puppy can help minimize the problem when they are adults. Both types of dysplasia are a result of the dog's hip and leg sockets being malformed, and that often leads to arthritis because the improper fit damages cartilage. The condition is possible to detect by the time a dog becomes an adult. The only way to detect it, though, is through X-rays.

Photo Courtesy of Amanda Unger

This is a problem that your Weimaraner may try to hide because he won't want to slow down. Your adult dog will walk a little more stiffly or may pant even when it's not hot. It usually becomes more obvious as a dog nears his golden years; similar to the way older people tend to change their gait to accommodate pain, your dog may do the same thing. Getting up may be a little more difficult in the beginning and will likely get worse as he ages.

While surgery is an option in severe cases, most dogs can benefit from less invasive treatment:

- Anti-inflammatory medications – Talk to your vet (dogs should not have large doses of anti-inflammatory drugs on a daily basis the way people do since aspirin and anti-inflammatories can damage your dog's kidneys.)
- Lower the amount of high-impact exercise your dog gets, especially on wood floors, tile, concrete, or other hard surfaces. Given how much your dog probably loves to swim, you can move more to a swimming exercise regimen to keep him active without the jarring motions of walking and jogging on hard surfaces.
- Joint fluid modifiers
- Physical therapy
- Weight loss (for dogs who are overweight or obese)

Spinal Dysraphism

This is a serious disease that is detectable at birth, so it is not likely that you will adopt a Weimaraner that has this problem from a good breeder. If you adopt from a less reputable breeder or a puppy mill, it is possible that you get a dog that has this serious condition.

Dogs that have spinal dysraphism usually have trouble walking because their spinal canal did not properly form. The problem is primarily with their back legs, which will mean that walking can be incredibly difficult for bigger dogs that have longer spines.

This disease can cause real problems for dogs, but they can still have very full lives since it is becoming increasingly easy for vets to provide equipment that can help dogs to get around with greater ease. There is no cure for it, but there are plenty of ways of boosting a dog's ability to move around your home and outdoors with much greater ease.

Hypertrophic Osteodystophy

Another ailment that is easily detected early, dogs with Hypertrophic Osteodystrophy will experience swelling in their bones when they are between four and six months old. The pain and discomfort can cause the dog to be irritable, as well as making it harder for them to move. In the most severe cases, they may be immobile.

There is no cure for this genetic disease, so treatment is largely geared toward helping you manage your Weimaraner's pain. Fortunately, as their bodies mature, the pain and swelling go away or is greatly reduced so that you and your Weimaraner can live a happy, full, active life.

Bloat/Gastric Dilatation and Volvulus (GDV)

> *A Weimaraner should have interest in its food and readily eat when fed—twice a day is best for digestion, minimizing gulping of food if the dog is really hungry. This will minimize excess air in the stomach, which can contribute to bloat, a life-threatening emergency that requires emergency surgery. It also allows you to pick up on any problems sooner.*
>
> **KYRA SCHLIEMAN**
> *SilverLining Weimaraners*

GDV, more commonly known as bloat, is a problem with dog breeds that have larger chests. Their stomach can fill with gases, causing the stomach to bloat. In the worst cases, the gas can cause the stomach to twist, cutting off the entrance and exit from the stomach. Nothing can enter or leave your dog's stomach once the stomach twists. While the bloat stage is not lethal, once the stomach twists, it can kill your dog.

Prevention is the best way of dealing with this problem. While you can have surgery done to keep the stomach from twisting, this may not be the best method of treatment for Weimaraners. You can reduce the risk of this problem by taking the following measures.

- Feed your dog two or three times a day (not just one meal)
- Add wet dog food to kibble (if you feed your dog commercial dog food)
- Ensure the dry dog food is calcium-rich

Chapter 17: Genetic Health Concerns Common to the Weimaraner

Skin Tumors

The sleek look of the Weimaraner does make it easier to detect issues on the skin, and skin tumors are definitely something that you will be able to see. It is unfortunately a common problem with this breed, with most of the tumors being hemangioma and hemangiosarcoma.

If you find lumps on your dog, get your dog to the vet as soon as possible to have it checked. It is likely nothing, but considering how much time you and your dog have probable spent outside together, you want to make sure that the problem isn't something serious.

Distichiasis

This ailment affects the dog's eyes, and the translation of the name means "double lashes." As this name indicates, the problem stems from the Weimaraner having two full rows of eyelashes on one eyelid. Though it can happen on the upper eyelid, the problem is usually occurs on the lower eyelid. In the worst cases, it can be all four eyelids, meaning your dog has eight rows of eyelashes that will definitely affect the dog's vision.

Photo Courtesy of Jennifer Lewitzki

It isn't a debilitating condition, but it can cause problems with the cornea, as well as making your dog have excessive tears forming in his eyes. Eye infections are incredibly common as well, with the problem potentially creating another problem, entropion. The vet has several options in treating the condition.

Entropion

Entropion is when the dog's eyelids roll inward, damaging the cornea as the eyelashes scratch it. The corrective surgery that fixes this problem can cause another eye disorder, ectropion. This is when the lower eyelid droops down so that you can see the soft pink tissue under the eye. While ectropion is not a serious problem—Basset Hounds live with it as a natural part of their facial structure—it does increase the likelihood of eye infections.

Common Owner Mistakes

In addition to genetic problems, there are things you can do that could unintentionally damage your dog's health; these mistakes are related to diet and exercise levels. In the puppy stage, it is a difficult balance to strike as your puppy is curious and enthusiastic. Even when he is a fully grown dog, you have to make sure you are minimizing how much stress is placed on your Weimaraner's body. Weight management is one important way of keeping your dog healthy. You need to balance your dog's diet with his level of activity to prevent exacerbation of hip and elbow dysplasia.

Failing to notice early signs of potential issues can be detrimental or even fatal to your Weimaraner. Any changes in your Weimaraner's behavior are likely a sign of something that should be checked by your vet.

> **HEALTH ALERT!**
> **Wobbler Syndrome**
>
> Wobbler syndrome affects many large-dog breeds, including Weimaraners, and results in a "wobbly" gait. Symptoms of this syndrome may be easier to see when dogs are walking on slippery surfaces, such as laminate or wood floors, and afflicted dogs may avoid these surfaces or express pain while walking across them. Research into this syndrome is ongoing, but there is no current consensus on where this disease originates and how it relates to genetics. However, a veterinarian can diagnose this syndrome and offer medical or surgical treatment options, depending on the severity of the disease.

Prevention and Monitoring

As mentioned in previous chapters, Weimaraners love to eat, but they really can't handle extra weight. The best way to help maintain your dog's health is to make sure he remains at a healthy weight. Checking your Weimaraner's weight is important and should be done at least once a quarter or twice a year. You and your vet should keep an eye on your dog's weight, as being overweight puts a strain on your dog's back, legs, joints, and muscles.

CHAPTER 18

The Aging Weimaraner

Even a high energy dog like the Weimaraner will slow down once the dog reaches those senior years. Granted, your Weimaraner may not want to slow down, so your work may be in trying to convince your dog not to try to be so active. Switching to more mentally stimulating work can help your dog to keep from injuring himself.

With a life expectancy between 11 and 14 years, Weimaraners tend to live longer than most other dogs their size. If you find a very conscientious breeder and take really good care of your dog, it's possible that your Weimaraner may live even longer than that. One breeder enthused about her eldest dog.

> *My dogs live to be very old. My old girl right now is 15 1/2 and she's doing very well. Physically she's in great shape but she may have a touch of dementia. I make sure she still gets exercise and she has all the comforts that an old dog should have. She's very happy!*
>
> CAMILLE RICE
> *Timberdoodle Weimaraners*

Weimaraners tend to start slowing between 7 and 9 years old, not that they will want you to notice. A dog may remain healthy his whole life, but his body still won't be able to do the same activities during the later years. For larger dogs, the decline often seems to happen a lot faster. The first signs are usually your dog's walking becoming a little

Chapter 18: The Aging Weimaraner

stiffer or when he starts panting more heavily earlier in the walk. If you see any of these signs, start shortening the walks. It's likely that your Weimaraner will want to continue to exercise as he ages, so you will need to either choose easier, shorter walks or start to include your dog in other kinds of activities.

Photo Courtesy of Jennifer Lewitzki

Your schedule is going to need to change as your canine slows down. You may need to monitor your Weimaraner's activity levels because he may get excited enough to hurt himself—that ability to focus may make him less aware of when he is hurting himself.

Regular vet visits, good but age-appropriate food, and lots of love are the things that your older dog really needs. Since this has probably been a pretty mellow dog for at least a few years now, you may already have a pretty good schedule set up. It may just be a matter of monitoring how much activity you guys enjoy. Watch your dog the next morning to make sure he isn't stiffer after spending a day out hiking or doing another more active or sustained activity.

There is a reason these are called the golden years—you can really enjoy them with your dog. You don't have to worry as much about him tearing things up out of boredom or getting overexcited on walks anymore. You can enjoy lazy evenings and peaceful weekends with some less strenuous exercise to break up the day. It's easy to make the senior years incredibly enjoyable for your Weimaraner and yourself by making the necessary adjustments.

Senior Care Challenges

In most cases, caring for an older dog is much simpler than taking care of a younger dog, and Weimaraners are no exception.

> *Love them to death. Your aging Weim is the most precious and dearest, they will need a safe floor to walk on (put down rugs on slippery floors). They may become deaf, so that silly sign language you used doing some of those early obedience classes will come in handy. Incontinence is to be expected, you may no longer be able to sleep with your best pal, so that's when those days of crating may come back in handy.*
>
> TONI FOW
> *Wing It Weimaraners*

Accommodations you should make for your senior Weimaraner include:

- Set water bowls out in a couple of different places so that your dog can easily reach them as needed. If your Weimaraner shows signs of having trouble drinking or eating, place slightly raised water dishes around the home.
- Cover hard floor surfaces (such as tile, hardwood, and vinyl). Use nonslip carpets or rugs.
- Add cushions and softer bedding for your Weimaraner. This will both make the surface more comfortable and help him stay warmer. There are bed warmers for dogs if your Weimaraner has achy joints or muscles. Of course, you also need to make sure he isn't too warm, so this can be a fine balancing act.
- To improve his circulation, increase how often you brush your Weimaraner.
- Stay inside in extreme heat and cold. Your Weimaraner is hardy, but an old canine cannot handle extreme changes as well as he once did.

- Use stairs or ramps for your Weimaraner wherever possible so that the old pup doesn't have to try to jump.
- Avoid moving your furniture around, particularly if your Weimaraner shows signs of having trouble with his sight or has dementia. A familiar home is more comforting and less stressful as your pet ages. If your Weimaraner isn't able to see as clearly as he once did, keeping the home familiar will make it easier for your dog to move around without getting hurt.
- If you have stairs, consider setting up an area where your dog can stay without having to go up and down the stairs too often.
- Create a space where your Weimaraner can relax with fewer distractions and noises. Don't make your old friend feel isolated, but do give him a place to get away from everyone if he needs to be alone.
- Be prepared to let your dog out more often for restroom breaks.

FUN FACT
A Grand Old Dog

The average life span of a Weimaraner is between 10 and 13 years. However, the oldest-recorded Wei-maraner reportedly lived for 18 years and ten months. Male dogs of this large breed typically reach a height of two to two and a half feet, while females are generally smaller. In addition, you can expect an adult male Weimaraner to weigh between 70 and 90 pounds and a female adult to reach 55 to 75 pounds.

Common Physical Disorders Related to Aging

Chapters 4 and 16 cover illnesses that are common or likely with a Weimaraner, but old age tends to bring a slew of ailments that aren't particular to any one breed. Here are the things you will need to watch for (as well as talk to your vet about).

- Diabetes is probably the greatest concern for a breed that loves to eat as much as your Weimaraner does, even with two hours of daily exercise most of the dog's adult life. Although diabetes is usually thought of as a genetic condition, any Weimaraner

can become diabetic if not fed and exercised properly. This is another reason why it's so important to be careful with your Weimaraner's diet and exercise levels.
- Arthritis is probably the most common ailment in any dog breed, and the Weimaraner is no exception. If your dog is showing signs of stiffness and pain after normal activities, talk with your vet about safe ways to help minimize the pain and discomfort of this common joint ailment.
- Gum disease is a common issue in older dogs as well, and you should be just as vigilant about brushing his teeth when your dog gets older as at any other age. A regular check of your Weimaraner's teeth and gums can help ensure this does not become a problem.
- Loss of eyesight or blindness is relatively common in older dogs, just as it is in humans. Have your dog's vision checked at least once a year and more often if it is obvious that his eyesight is failing.
- Kidney disease is a common problem in older dogs and one that you should monitor the older your Weimaraner gets. If your canine is drinking more often and having accidents regularly, get your Weimaraner to the vet as soon as possible and have him checked for kidney disease.

Steps and Ramps

You shouldn't pick your large Weimaraner up to carry him upstairs or put him in the car. Steps and ramps are the best way to safely ensure your Weimaraner can maintain some level of self-sufficiency as he ages. Also, using steps and ramps provides a bit of extra exercise.

If your Weimaraner has trouble seeing, you will need to make sure that you assist your dog up into cars or other inclines so that he doesn't get hurt. This can be difficult because your dog likely won't want to be less agile than in earlier years, so be supportive and give your dog a lot of praise so he knows that he's doing very well. Not only will your dog feel better about the lost abilities, it will be a great reminder that he's still very much a loved dog.

Chapter 18: The Aging Weimaraner

Photo Courtesy of Sherri Hightower

Vet Visits

As your Weimaraner ages, you are going to notice the slowdown, and the pains in your Weimaraner's body are going to be obvious, just like they are in an older person. You need to make sure that you have regular visits with your vet to ensure you aren't doing anything that could potentially harm your Weimaraner. If your Weimaraner has a debilitating ailment or condition, you may want to discuss options for ensuring a better quality of life, such as wheels if your Weimaraner's legs begin to have serious issues.

The Importance of Regular Vet Visits

> *I really like getting a veterinarian who does chiropractic care. Adjustment and acupuncture are very helpful as dogs age. Aging Weimaraners are awesome. They are so loving.*
>
> **MARY CERNAK**
> *Weimaraner Breeder*

Just as humans go to visit the doctor more often as they age, you'll need to take your dog to see your vet with greater frequency. The vet can make sure that your Weimaraner is staying active without overdoing it and that there is no unnecessary stress on your older dog. If your canine has sustained an injury and hidden it from you, your vet is more likely to detect it.

Your vet can also make recommendations about activities and changes to your schedule based on your Weimaraner's physical abilities and any changes in personality. For example, if your Weimaraner is panting more now, it could be a sign of pain from stiffness. This could be difficult to distinguish given how much Weimaraners pant as a rule, but if you see other signs of pain, schedule a visit with the vet. Your vet can help you determine the best way to keep your Weimaraner happy and active during the later years.

What to Expect at Vet Visits

- Your vet is going to talk about your dog's history, even if you have visited every year. This talk is necessary to see how things have gone or if any possible problems have started to show or have gotten worse.
- While you chat, your vet will probably conduct a complete physical examination to assess your dog's health.
- Depending on how old your dog is and the kind of health he is in, your vet may want to run different tests. The following are some of the most common tests for older dogs.
  - ☐ Arthropod-borne disease testing, which involves drawing blood and testing it for viral infections
  - ☐ Chemistry screening for kidney, liver, and sugar evaluation
  - ☐ Complete blood count
  - ☐ Fecal flotation, which involves mixing your dog's poop with a special liquid to test for worms and other parasites
  - ☐ Heartworm testing
  - ☐ Urinalysis, which tests your dog's urine to check the health of your dog's kidneys and urinary system
- The same routine wellness check that the vet has been conducting on your dog all his life
- Any breed-specific tests for your aging Weimaraner

Changes to Watch for

Keep an eye out for different signs that your dog is slowing down. This will help you to know when to adjust the setup around your home and to reduce how much your old pup is exercising.

Appetite and Nutritional Requirements

> "
> *A good supplement for an aging Weim is Cosequin for joint health. Also, any lumps that may appear should not be too concerning unless they grow large or appear painful.*
>
> JOE WIDOMSKI
> *Shade of Grey Weimaraners*
> "

With less exercise, your dog doesn't need as many calories, which means you need to adjust your pup's diet. If you opt to feed your Weimaraner commercial dog food, make sure you change to a senior food.

If you make your Weimaraner's food, talk to your vet and take the time to research how best to reduce calories without sacrificing taste. Your canine is going to need less fat in his food, so you may need to find something healthier that still has a lot of taste to supplement the types of foods you gave your Weimaraner as a puppy or active adult dog.

Exercise

> "
> *If orthopedic issues arise, not having your dog use the stairs or hike uphill will be appreciated by him, although he will do it because he's a Weimaraner and you've asked him to; remember—your dog wants to please you!*
>
> KYRA SCHLIEMAN
> *SilverLining Weimaraners*
> "

Since Weimaraners are so gregarious, they are going to be just as happy with extra attention from you as they were with exercise when they were younger. If you make fewer demands, decrease the number of walks, or in any way change the routine, your Weimaraner will quickly adapt to the new program. You will need to make those changes based on your dog's ability, so it's up to you to adjust the schedule and keep your Weimaraner happily active. Shorter, more frequent walks should take care of your Weimaraner's exercise needs, as well as help to break up your day a little more.

Your dog will enjoy napping as much as walking, especially if he gets to cuddle with you. Sleeping beside you while you watch television or as you nap is pretty much all it takes to make your older Weimaraner content, but he still needs to exercise.

The way your Weimaraner slows down will probably be the hardest part of watching him age. You may notice that your Weimaraner spends more time sniffing during walks, which could be a sign that your dog is tiring. It could also be his way of acknowledging that long steady walks are a thing of the past, and so he is stopping to enjoy the little things more. Stopping to smell things may now give him the excitement that he used to get by walking farther.

While you should be watching for your dog to tire, he may also let you know. If he is walking slower, looking up at you, and flopping down, that could be his way of letting you know it's time to return home. If your canine can't manage long walks, make the walks shorter and more numerous and spend more time romping around your yard or home with your buddy.

Aging and the Senses

> *The senior Weimaraner continues to benefit from regular exercise, albeit at a slower pace as it ages. It should not be overweight. Careful with introducing new things (kids, grandkids, new pets, or a new home or vehicle) to a dog that doesn't hear or see well; it can startle the dog.*
>
> **KYRA SCHLIEMAN**
> *SilverLining Weimaraners*

Just like people, dogs' senses weaken as they get older, and larger dogs' senses tend to deteriorate faster than smaller dogs. They won't hear things as well as they used to, they won't see things as clearly, and their sense of smell will weaken.

The following are some of the signs that your dog is losing at least one of his senses.

- It becomes easy to surprise or startle your dog. You need to be careful because this can make your Weimaraner aggressive, a scary prospect even in old age. Do NOT sneak up on your old dog, as this can be bad for both of you, and he deserves better than to be scared.
- Your dog may seem to ignore you because he is less responsive when you issue a command. If you have not had a problem before, your dog isn't being stubborn; he is likely losing his hearing.
- Cloudy eyes may be a sign of loss of sight, though it does not mean that your dog is blind.

If your dog seems to be "behaving badly," it is a sign that he is aging, not that he doesn't care or wants to rebel. Do not punish your older dog.

Adjust your schedule to meet your dog's changing abilities. Adjust water bowl height, refrain from rearranging rooms, and pet your dog more often. He is probably nervous about losing his abilities, so it is up to you to comfort him.

Keeping Your Senior Dog Mentally Active

> *When they are slowing down, continue the daily walks, slower or shorter, but it's extremely good for their mental stability. Continue with some training that isn't too physically hard on your dog, like nose work, and keep taking it to dog-friendly places.*
>
> CHRISTINE GRISELL
> *Nani's Weimaraners*

Just because your Weimaraner can't walk as far doesn't mean that his brain isn't just as focused and capable. As he slows down physically, focus more on activities that are mentally stimulating. As long as your Weimaraner has all of the basics down, you can teach him all kinds of low-impact tricks. At this point, training could be easier because your Weimaraner has learned to focus better, and he'll be happy to have something he can still do with you.

New toys are another great way to help keep your dog's mind active. Be careful that the toys aren't too rough on your dog's older jaw and teeth. Tug-of-war may be a game of the past (you don't want to hurt old teeth), but other games, such as hide-and-seek, will still be very much appreciated. Whether you hide toys or yourself, this can be a game that keeps your Weimaraner guessing. There are also food balls, puzzles, and other games that focus on cognitive abilities.

Some senior dogs suffer from cognitive dysfunction (CCD) syndrome, a type of dementia. It is estimated that 85% of all cases of dementia in dogs go undiagnosed because of the difficulty in pinpointing the problem. It manifests more as a problem of temperament.

If your dog begins to act differently, you should take him to the vet to see if he has CCD. While there really isn't any treatment for it, your vet can recommend things you can do to help your dog. Things like rearranging the rooms of your home are strongly discouraged, as familiarity with his surroundings will help your dog feel more comfortable and will reduce stress as he loses his cognitive abilities. Mental stimulation will help to fight CCD, but you should plan to keep your dog mentally stimulated regardless of whether or not he exhibits symptoms of dementia.

Advantages to the Senior Years

The last years of your Weimaraner's life can be just as enjoyable (if not more so) than the earlier stages since your dog will have mellowed. All of those high-energy activities will give way to cuddles and relaxation. Having your pup just enjoy your company can be incredibly nice (just remember to keep up his activity levels instead of getting too complacent with your Weimaraner's newfound love of resting and relaxing.)

Photo Courtesy of Charlene Yablonsky

Your Weimaraner will continue to be a loving companion, interacting with you at every opportunity—that does not change with age. Your canine's limitations should dictate interactions and activities. If you are busy, make sure you schedule time with your Weimaraner to do things that are within those limitations. It is just as easy to make an older Weimaraner happy as it is with a young one, and it is easier on you since relaxing is more essential to your old friend.

Preparing to Say Goodbye

This is something that all dog parents (well, pet parents, really) don't want to think about, but as you watch your Weimaraner slow down, you will know that your time with your sweet pup is coming to an end. Most working dogs tend to suddenly decline, making it very obvious when you need to start taking extra care of their aging bodies. They have trouble on smoother surfaces or can't walk nearly as far as they once did. It's certainly sad, but when it starts to happen, you know to begin to prepare to say goodbye.

Some dogs can continue to live for years after they begin to slow down, but most working dogs don't make it more than about a year or two. Sometimes dogs will lose their interest in eating, will have a stroke, or other problems will arise with little warning. Eventually, it will be time to say goodbye, whether at home or at the vet's office. You need to be prepared, and that is exactly why you should be making the most of these last few years.

Talk to your family about how you will care for your dog over the last few years or months of his life. Many dogs will be perfectly happy, despite their limited abilities. Some may begin to have problems controlling their bowel movements, while others may have problems getting up from a prone position. There are solutions to all of these problems. It is key to remember that quality of life should be the primary consideration, and since your dog cannot tell you how he feels, you will have to take cues from your dog. If your dog still seems happy, there is no reason to euthanize him.

At this stage, your dog is probably perfectly happy just sleeping near you for 18 hours a day. That is fine as long as he still gets excited about walking, eating, and being petted. The purpose of euthanasia is to reduce suffering, not to make things more convenient for yourself. This is what makes the decision so difficult, but your dog's behavior should be a fairly good indicator of how he is feeling. Here are some other things to watch to help you evaluate your dog's quality of life:

- Appetite
- Drinking
- Urinating and defecation
- Pain (noted by excessive panting)
- Stress levels
- Desire to be active or with family (if your dog wants to be alone most of the time, that is usually a sign that he is trying to be alone for the end)

Talk to your vet if your dog has a serious illness to determine what the best path forward is. They can provide the best information on the quality of your dog's life and how long your dog is likely to live with the disease or ailment.

If your dog gets to the point when you know that he is no longer happy, he can't move around, or he has a fatal illness, it is probably time to say goodbye. This is a decision that should be made as a family, always putting the dog's needs and quality of life first. If you decide it is time to say goodbye, determine who will be present at the end.

Once at the vet's office, if you have decided to euthanize the dog, you can make the last few minutes very happy by feeding your dog the things he couldn't eat before. Things like chocolate and grapes can put a smile on his face for the remaining time he has.

You can also have your dog euthanized at home. If you decide to request a vet to come to your home, be prepared for additional charges for the home visit. You also need to determine where you want your dog to be, whether inside or outside, and in which room if you decide to do it inside.

Make sure at least one person is present so that your dog is not alone during the last few minutes of his life. You don't want your dog to die surrounded by strangers. The process is fairly peaceful, but your dog will probably be a little stressed. He will pass within a few minutes of the injection. Continue to talk to him as his brain will continue to work even after his eyes close.

Once your dog is gone, you need to determine what to do with the body.

- Cremation is one of the most common ways of taking care of your pet's body. You can get an urn or request a container to scatter your dog's ashes over his favorite places. Make sure you don't dump his ashes in places where that is not permitted. Private cremation is more expensive than communal cremation, but it means that the only ashes you get are from your dog. Communal creation occurs when several pets are cremated together.
- Burial is the easiest method if you have your pet euthanized at home, but you need to check your local regulations to ensure that you can bury your dog at home, as this is illegal in some places. You also need to consider the soil. If your yard is rocky or sandy, that will create problems. Also, don't bury your pet in your yard if it is near wells that people use as a drinking source or if it is near wetlands or waterways. Your dog's body can contaminate the water as it decays. You can also look into a pet cemetery if there is one in your area.

Grief and Healing

Dogs become members of our families, so their passing can be incredibly difficult. People go through all of the same emotions and feelings of loss with a dog as they do with close friends and family. The absence of that presence in your life is jarring, especially with such a loving, loyal dog like the Weimaraner. Your home is a constant reminder of the loss, and in the beginning, you and your family will probably feel considerable grief. Saying goodbye is going to be difficult. Taking a couple of days off work is not a bad idea. While people who don't have dogs will say that your Weimaraner was just a dog, you know better, and it is okay to feel the pain and to grieve as you would for any lost loved one.

Losing your Weimaraner is also going to make a substantial change in your schedule. It will likely take a while to get accustomed to the way your schedule has shifted. Fight the urge to go out and get a new dog because you almost certainly are not ready yet.

Everyone grieves differently, so you will need to allow yourself to grieve in a way that is healthy for you. Everyone in your family will feel the loss differently, too, so let them feel it in their own ways. Some people don't require much time, while others can feel the loss for months. There is no timetable, so you can't try to force it on yourself or any member of your family.

Talk about how you would like to remember your pup. You can have a memorial for your lost pet, tell stories, or plant a tree in your dog's memory. If someone doesn't want to participate, that is fine.

Try to return to your normal routine as much as possible if you have other pets. This can be both painful and helpful as your other pets will still need you just as much (especially other dogs who have also lost their companion).

If you find that grief is hindering your ability to function normally, seek professional help. If needed, you can go online to find support groups in your area to help you and your family, especially if this was your first dog. Sometimes it helps to talk about the loss so that you can start to heal.